PM 101

According to the
Olde Curmudgeon

AN INTRODUCTION TO THE
BASIC CONCEPTS OF
MODERN PROJECT MANAGEMENT

FRANCIS M. WEBSTER JR.

PROJECT MANAGEMENT INSTITUTE

Library of Congress Cataloging-in-Publication Data

Webster, Francis Marion.
    PM 101: according to the Olde Curmudgeon : an introduction to the basic con-
cepts of modern project management / Francis M. Webster, Jr.
       p.   cm.
    Revised and expanded articles which first appeared as "PM 101" in PM network,
the Institute's journal, with additional chapters written for this volume.
    Includes bibliographical references and index.
    ISBN: 1-880410-55-9 (pbk. : alk. paper)
    1. Industrial project management.   I. Project Management Institute.   II. Title.
HD69.P75W425 2000
658.4'04 – – dc21   99–41261
                                                          CIP

3 2280 00722 6087

ISBN: 1-880410-55-9

Published by: Project Management Institute, Inc.
                Four Campus Boulevard
                Newtown Square, Pennsylvania 19073-3299 USA
                Phone: 610-356-4600 or Visit our website: www.pmi.org

10 9 8 7 6 5 4 3 2 1

Dedication

To my wife of forty-seven years, whose
forbearance and encouragement have allowed
me to be involved in this "crazy" profession.

Contents

Figures

Tables

Foreword

Note from the Olde Curmudgeon: Differing from standard publishing practice, this Foreword has been written by three individuals because of their different and essential perspectives on project management: Dave Cleland, the strategic and conceptual; Hans Thamhain, the technology research and consulting; and Les Prudhomme, the practitioner.

PM 101 According to the Olde Curmudgeon is a significant contribution to the literature of project management. Fran Webster offers the book as an introduction to the basic concepts of modern project management—and he delivers just that in this readable and enjoyable book.

The timing for this book is just right. There have been several hundred books published on project management—these books offer many different treatments of the discipline. Not many of them provide a clear and fundamental examination of the basic concepts and processes of project management. The strength of this book is that it provides sufficient information and basic explanations on how to manage projects.

The root cause of failure—and success—in the management of projects depends on how well the basic concepts and processes of project management have been carried out by the project manager in managing and leading the project stakeholders. Failure is seldom caused by some esoteric factor—rather failure is caused by the lack of sound, basic project management principles and processes. This is why mastery of the basics of the discipline as put forth in this book is so important.

Anyone involved in the management of projects should find this book quite useful. The range of chapter topics includes some that are particular noteworthy—

and usually not found in competitive books. The author's treatment of the technical and administrative skills of the project manager, as well as project leadership ideas, provides valuable insight into the discipline. Young professionals entering the field of project management should find the clear presentation of the basics of the discipline in this book useful. "Oldtimers," who need reinforcement of their knowledge, skills, and attitudes in project management, will find value in a careful perusal of this excellent book.

David Cleland, Ernest E. Roth Professor, University of Pittsburgh

PM 101 represents a refreshing and much different approach to other books on project management. It is about the principals of modern project management and how to apply them effectively in today's demanding project environment. As project operations have become highly complex, both in concept and in practice, it is delightful to see the issues being brought into perspective. What we need is not to invent more tools, but to use the ones that we have effectively. *PM 101* skillfully summarizes the concept, tools, and techniques of modern project management that have stood the test of time, and have become threshold competencies for project management professionals today. Yet, Francis Webster does not stop with the principals. He offers great perspective, integrating the processes and metrics with the human side of modern project management. Filled with anecdotes of contemporary project management practice, *PM 101* tells the reader how to get into the proper frame of mind for becoming an effective project management professional who understands the concepts, tools, and processes, and can adapt them to today's dynamic project scenarios.

From my perspective as researcher and practitioner of project management, I appreciate Webster's perspective and integration of the human side of project management, ranging from communications to leadership, negotiations, and team building. I have seen firsthand how difficult it is for project leaders in today's lean, flexible, and power-shared organizations to deal with the human issues that drive important success factors such as resource commitment, creativity, buy-in, and. ultimately, project performance.

PM 101 pulls together many threads from different domains of established project management knowledge and best practice. Clearly, Webster's book deserves careful reading by all project management professionals.

Hans J. Thamhain, PMP, Ph.D., Bentley College

You've heard the expression, "Yesterday I couldn't spell 'Project Manager.' Today I are one." Now what? You've just been assigned to manage a project, which is part of a larger business initiative being managed by one of the company's senior managers. Your manager referred to your part as a "project" and called you a "project manager." What do you do now? Where do you start? What is project management?

Fran Webster, the Olde Curmudgeon, has taken his years of experience in the field of project management and condensed it into a basic primer on the subject. Fran recognized that, while many books have been written on project management in general and on the many different specific aspects of project management, there was a need for a starting point for someone new to the field or someone needing a basic understanding of project management. Well, here it is. This easy-reading primer won't make you a project manager, but it will provide you with a basic understanding of what project management is all about and will get you started in the right direction.

Les Prudhomme, PMP, Associate Director,
Construction Industry Institute

Preface

This book started as a series of tutorial articles aimed at answering Sam's question (What do I do now?) and guiding every Sam through the experience and anxiety of learning to deal with the ambiguity, uncertainty, conflict, leadership, and all other privileges of being a project manager. The articles, originally published as PM 101 in past issues of *PM Network®*, have been revised and supplemented to include information that was precluded by size limitations in the original articles. Some have benefited from further consideration since that time. It is hoped that these chapters will be found useful for those who want to learn about the concepts and practice of modern project management (MPM). Perhaps it will also be useful to others interested in the ideas, concepts, and benefits of using MPM. *PM 102*, to be published in 2000, completes the originally anticipated series.

Modern project management is a term that was promoted in *PM Network* while I was editor-in-chief for the Project Management Institute (PMI®). The need for a descriptor of PMI came about as follows. I could imagine walking into the office of an old-timer, perhaps with the title of vice president of manufacturing, and saying, "Sir, you really ought to start using project management." Still having an image of myself as being a *young whippersnapper*, I could imagine this old-timer saying something like, "What the hell are you trying to tell me? I've been doing projects all my professional life. Don't you think I've been managing those projects?" The monologue would go on and on, depending on how deeply I had gored his ox. So I started promoting the term, modern project management. That way, I would be insulting him a little more subtly, and maybe he would allow me to say something more before he threw me out of his office.

Well, all the time that I used the term, I was asking myself, "Okay, what do you say next? What do you mean by that?" Like so many other things in my professional career, I never really had time to think about it very thoroughly. Now that I am retired (and can no longer deny that I am an old-timer), I've had time to ponder and believe that at last I have some answers to the question, which may be found largely in Chapter III, Modern Project Management. Perhaps you have a better approach; if so, I would be happy to hear about it.

THE OLDE CURMUDGEON

The Olde Curmudgeon (OC) first came on the scene in an article published in *Project Management Journal* (1984) and was prefaced by the following caveat:

> This is the first of a series of commentaries proffered by "The Olde Curmudgeon." The purpose of these memos to the editor is to be a thorn in the side of the confident and comfortable project manager, to ask questions that even your own best friend won't ask (like, "Why isn't your deodorant working?") and to invite a dialogue to challenge both the conventional wisdom of practitioners and puncture the theories of sanctimonious academicians who have never had to make their theories work. The opinions set forth are solely the responsibility of The Olde Curmudgeon and do not necessarily reflect the position of the Editor or of the *Project Management Journal*.

Thus, the OC is a salty character who may have coined the phrase, "Been there, done that!" He is willing to share his accumulated wisdom, if you are willing to endure his anecdotes and callused attitude. The wisdom of the OC should be applied with some caution, as it can have unintended consequences. Nevertheless, he would say something like, "Forewarned is forearmed!"

While serving as editor-in-chief for PMI, I sensed a need for some articles discussing project management at a rather basic level. After all, most of the articles presumed the reader was familiar with previous project management literature. Also, it seemed that these articles should approach the subject in a practical sense, incorporating some lessons seldom discussed in academic classrooms. These lessons are often learned at the *school of hard knocks*. Perhaps they will help you avoid a few bruises along the way.

COMPUTERS

Little mention or use is made in this book of computer software available to manage projects. This is done purposely, in part because of a long-held belief that you should never use computer applications to do something that you do not understand and cannot first do yourself.

The greatest contribution of computers is their ability to process lots of data very quickly; thus, they are very useful for managing realistic-sized projects. They have gained fame on large projects but are often very useful on small projects, especially if there are several of them. Sometimes, the problems get to be so large that it simply overwhelms the human mind to comprehend them. Nevertheless, these problems are solved by many simple calculations, each of which can be well understood.

Perhaps the greatest value of computers is in managing the resources used on one or more projects. Hiring and firing costs often are substantial. Scheduling too much work to be done at one time in a specific area can result in considerable inefficiencies.

Care should be exercised in using project management software. You should take special care to understand exactly how it solves certain resource-scheduling problems, as it may use a decision rule that is undesirable for your project.

Updating the schedule for actual performance and adapting to change is much easier once the original data are on the computer.

These are just some of the values of using computers. The first step is to truly understand what they are programmed to do.

ABOUT SAM

Sam is a fictional character with whom you might be able to empathize. You can decide if Sam is short for Samuel or Samantha! It is not unusual for people to get their first taste of project management in much the same manner as Sam does: by being thrown into the water and left to swim. Follow Sam's adventures in learning about MPM.

Acknowledgments

The Olde Curmudgeon accepts responsibility and apologizes for any shortcoming in this book. Most evident is that he has not actually worked on projects in the newer virtual team or even in the modern real-time computer environment. Thus, anyone operating in these environments should consider how to adapt the concepts contained herein, which should be considered advanced study and can be assisted by the many good articles that have appeared in PMI publications and by attending local, national, and international meetings.

It would be impossible to give either specific citations for all the information contained in this book or to recognize all those who contributed to the Olde Curmudgeon's *education* over the years. The articles and books cited are for the benefit of the reader, to delve further into these fine sources.

Special thanks are given to Dave Cleland, Hans Thainhaim, and Les Prudhomme for taking the time to read the manuscript and make suggestions.

Appreciation is expressed to PMI for permission to use material contained in *A Guide to the Project Management Body of Knowledge* and other publications, such as the Mars Pathfinder Project submitted for the PMI 1998 Project of the Year by the Jet Propulsion Laboratory. Paraphrased excerpts from this document appear in the appendices at the end of some of the chapters.

Chapter I

Modern Project Management— Its Time Has Come!

In the beginning there was the word, and the word was DOIT. Thus, the first project manager received an assignment. This project manager was named Sam. Sam's reaction was normal for the species: "Golly gee, what do I do now? We don't do projects!"

Perhaps the applicant for the housekeeping position can state, "I don't do windows!", and still get the job. However, today's manager or executive who says, "I don't do projects!", is in trouble. Business literature is replete with articles promoting flatter organizations, the team approach to management, concurrent engineering, reduced time to market, and empowering employees. All of these are synonymous with the application of, are inherent in, or are best accomplished with the aid of modern project management (MPM). Indeed, it is suggested that most executives spend more of their time concerned with work being performed in the project mode than in any other mode. In general, executives are concerned about the future products and capabilities of the organization—i.e., the corporate strategy, which is implemented through projects. Successful implementation of corporate strategy is

1

therefore dependent on successful project management. Thus, the successful executive must not only comprehend projects and project managers, but also must be skilled in managing them.

Although receiving less publicity than the new concepts of total quality management, material requirements planning, and just-in-time management, another *revolution* has been growing in importance in the last forty years: planning, scheduling, and controlling project work. This new concept in management dates back to the mid-fifties and has been characterized by varying degrees of interest and understanding. Today, it is the basis for a major portion of economic activity: the management of change. It has developed from being a very specialized technique to a management philosophy supported by a variety of techniques, concepts, and theories.

One way to judge the relevance of a new concept is to consider where and how frequently it is mentioned in publications. In recent years, articles have been appearing more frequently in journals, such as *Fortune* and *Harvard Business Review*. The popular management author and speaker, Tom Peters, refers to project management extensively in his books: *Liberation Management* (1996) and *The Circle of Innovation: You Can't Shrink Your Way to Greatness* (1998).

Project management has progressed to a point of being recognized as a distinct career and profession. Project managers are served by two major professional societies—the Project Management Institute (PMI®) with worldwide membership, the International Project Management Association (IPMA, formerly INTERNET, and principally in Europe), and several other similar organizations, primarily oriented to the interests of single nations. Among other activities, these societies have staged meetings, conducted training and education programs, certified project management professionals, and accredited academic programs in project management.

Many people have adopted a stereotypical view of project management as being applicable to very large projects, especially in construction and defense/aerospace. Although it has been very valuable in these industries, it also has been used extensively in the pharmaceutical, automotive, utility, communications, and many other industries, as well as in product development, information systems, and other functional areas. It has been used for athletic events, including the Olympic Games, and for movie productions. More recently, network planning has found its way into the executive suite as a convenient way to express corporate strategic plans, including alternative methods to achieve corporate objectives.

Indeed, it is difficult to imagine an industry or functional area of business for which MPM would not prove useful. Even in the most repetitive of industries and functions, there is change that must be managed. Wherever there is change to be managed, there is an opportunity to accomplish that change more efficiently and effectively through the use of MPM.

WHAT ARE PROJECTS?

> Along the way to this assignment, Sam had gained experience on some smaller efforts, which many will recognize as Honey-dos, as in, "Honey, do this, and honey, do that." These efforts, each of increasing magnitude, have prepared Sam for this even larger project—to create a means for crossing a river!

There are many ways to think about projects. They can be described in many ways, and they can be defined differently. Perhaps this is why there has been so much ambiguity about and lack of appreciation for project management.

Projects can be described by example. Most such descriptions start with things such as the Pyramids, the Great Wall of China, and other undertakings of ancient history. These were major construction projects and, of course, construction is inherently a project-oriented industry. A modern construction project that rivals all others is the English Channel Tunnel, a $12 billion effort that opened in 1994 (Lemley 1992).

There are other project-oriented industries, not the least of which is the pharmaceutical industry. The search for new drugs has led to a remarkably high level of health and life expectancy. The aerospace industry is noted for its accomplishments not only in space, but also for the technological developments that have changed the way we live and work.

But not all projects are of such magnitude. Remodeling or redecorating a house is certainly a project. A community fundraising campaign is a project. A political campaign is a project. Developing a new product, developing the advertising program to promote that product, and training the sales and support staff to effectively move and service the product are all projects. Responding to an Environmental Protection Agency complaint is a project, particularly if the complaint is substantial. It is probable that most executives spend more of their time planning and monitoring *changes*—i.e., projects—in their organizations than they do maintaining the status quo.

Some Characteristics of Projects

> The other side of the river was abundant with food; it was greener, and it was safer. Thus, Sam's client was anxious to get to the other side. Indeed, it was during this project that the query, "Are we almost there yet?", was first coined. Sam was learning about the role and nature of stakeholders in projects.

Projects are the change efforts of society. The pace of change, in whatever dimension, has been increasing at an ever-faster rate. The only way organizations can survive in this modern world is through effective and efficient management of change efforts.

Projects are ubiquitous. They are everywhere; everybody does them. If they are so common, why all the fuss? Very simply, better ways of managing projects have been and are being developed. Organizations that take the lead in implementing these capabilities will consistently perform their projects better, and be more competitive in general.

The project is not synonymous with the product of the project. The word *project* is often used ambiguously, sometimes referring to the project and sometimes referring to the product of the project. This is not a trivial distinction, as both entities have characteristics unique unto themselves. The project is the process by which the product is produced. The project is intended to end—i.e., to have a finite life. The product of the project is generally intended to have a long—i.e., more nearly infinite—life.

Projects are composed of activities. They are usually nonrepetitive, operating on an interrelated set of items that have inherent technologically determined relationships. For example, one activity must be completed before another can begin. Generally, these technological relationships are very difficult to violate without changing the plan or the design of the product. For example, if getting yourself dressed is considered a project, there is a technological relationship between putting on your socks and putting on your shoes. Whether you put on both socks and then both shoes, or complete the left foot before the right foot, is a question of preference. In MPM, a project network diagram is used to portray these technological sequences.

Projects involve multiple resources—both human and nonhuman— that require close coordination. Generally, there is a variety of resources, each with its own unique technologies, skills, and traits. Not only is there a varied mix of resources, but also the mix changes over time, and the total units of resources used changes over time. These varied approaches lead to an inherent characteristic of projects: conflict. There is conflict between resources regarding concepts, theory, techniques, and so on. There is conflict for resources as to quantity, timing, and specific assignments, and there are many other sources of conflict in projects. Thus, a project manager must be skilled in managing conflict.

Projects are unique undertakings. They generally result in a single unit of output. There are more economical ways to manage production of multiple units of a product. The installation of an entertainment center by a homeowner with the help of a few friends is a project. The objective is to complete the installation and enjoy the product of the effort. The homeowner is not likely to repeat this process frequently. It is not unusual, however, for multiple units to be involved in a project at one level of detail or another. A high-rise building typically involves multiple floors, each of which is nearly alike. Installing the windows in such a building certainly involves multiple units.

Careful examination of the activities comprising a project discloses that many of them are rather routine and performed frequently in the organization. Often 10 percent or less are unique. Nevertheless, because the products of different projects are seldom the same, the specific manner in which the activities are combined, their work content, and other such characteristics of activities result in the total project being unique.

Projects come in all sizes. Size does not determine whether a work effort is a project or not. Size only impacts the degree and extent to which the techniques and principles of project management are employed. Organizations benefit from standardizing many practices of project management, but differentiate the intensity of application as a function of size, importance of the project to the organization, and the nature and availability of the resources to be employed. This standardized approach aids in the orderly development of project management personnel in a consistent and efficient manner.

Managerial emphasis is on timely accomplishment of the project. This differs from managerial emphases on other modes of work. For example, efficiency is generally not the major objective. A need exists for the resulting product of the project; otherwise, the project would not have been authorized. Most projects require the investment of considerable sums of money prior to enjoyment of the benefits of the resulting product. Interest on these funds is a major reason for emphasis on time. Being first in the market often determines long-term market position, creating time pressure; thus, time is of the essence. This time pressure, combined with the need to coordinate multiple resources, explains why most *project management systems* have emphasized time management.

> Sam yearned for a better way to get to the objective of the project faster. After all, even the most patient, dedicated project manager grows weary of repeated queries such as, "Are we almost there yet?" But, alas, it was many, many generations of Sams later before the development of MPM.

THE DEVELOPMENT OF MODERN PROJECT MANAGEMENT

The most-publicized first developments in MPM planning and scheduling were sponsored by duPont (Kelley Jr. and Walker 1989) and the

United States (U.S.) Navy (Malcolm et al. 1959), followed closely by the U.S. Department of Defense and National Aeronautical and Space Administration. Recent research on the history of MPM suggests that the first use of "concurrency" in managing projects was by General Bernard Schriever, who was assigned responsibility for developing the first intercontinental ballistic missile by the U.S. Air Force in 1954. A manual precursor of the program evaluation and review technique was developed at about the same time, called performance evaluation program. These efforts gave the impression that the techniques were applicable to construction and maintenance (in the case of duPont) and very large-scale defense and space-systems development. Many management book authors reinforced this impression. With the advent of a variety of microcomputer-based project-scheduling software, and the availability and convenience of use of these packages, projects of all sizes have benefited from their application.

In the early years of MPM, the cost of application for project-scheduling software was substantial for several reasons. The development of MPM has paralleled the development of computers. Early computers and software programs were primitive and expensive. The first project management systems were not user friendly. These techniques were inherently labor-intensive and required considerable computer expertise to use. Today, both of these deficiencies have been overcome. User-friendliness has enabled novice users to use significant features of a package with only a couple of hours of introduction— generally from the user's manual, help messages, or online tutoring programs. Training in the use of project management techniques has become widespread. Many persons with project management responsibilities find it easy to plan their projects in an interactive mode, which has provided considerable benefit with a better understanding of the project and more accurate communication of the desired approach for the execution of the project.

Most managers and engineers have been involved in and managed projects. The degree and scope of responsibility assigned to these individuals has typically been rather limited, often with responsibility shifting from one individual to another as the project progresses through its various phases. Today, it is more common for an individual to be given responsibility for managing the project from its inception to its closure.

Thus, many changes have taken place in the management of projects. While project management may have seemed to be almost entirely the application of network-based scheduling techniques, today the use of these techniques for planning, scheduling, and controlling can be considered, at most, to comprise 10 percent of MPM. Behavioral considerations, contract management, risk management, and other concepts have been recognized as increasingly significant. Perhaps the appropriate view is that planning and scheduling techniques have improved in both usability and usefulness to such an extent that the project manager and the project management team are able to perform planning and control functions in much less time and effort. This affords them the time to also perform the other functions much better. Appropriate training in these broader issues of MPM cannot be learned from a user's manual, help messages, or online tutoring programs.

> One scenario is that Sam finally completed a raft after several false starts. However, the project was completed late and over budget, and there were numerous complaints that the raft, as built, was not exactly what the client really had in mind. Nevertheless, the stakeholders were grateful, because Sam had still maintained a brilliant record of completing projects in a manner that exceeded expectations of that era.
>
> What might Sam have done differently? In the following chapters, we will explore some ideas and techniques that would have helped Sam bring this project in on time, within budget, and meeting or exceeding the client's expectations, a more favorable scenario.

BENEFITS OF MODERN PROJECT MANAGEMENT

The benefits of MPM have been reported in article after article in PMI's *PM Network®* magazine and its *Project Management Journal*, as well as its annual seminar/symposium *Proceedings*. Just a few of them are discussed here.

The development of the *Endicott Oil Field* production facility, the first offshore oil field north of the Arctic Circle, was accomplished at a substantial saving of both time and cost. Although many of the facilities were produced on-site, using contractors experienced in that milieu, the major process unit was built in Louisiana, moved on a one hundred-by-four hundred-foot barge down the Mississippi River, through the Panama Canal and the Bering Strait, and off-loaded onto the manmade main production island. This had to be accomplished within a six-week window when the Arctic Ocean was not frozen, or else the project would be delayed by a year (Flones 1987).

The *Voyager 2 Deep Space Project* involved three major agencies—1) National Science Foundation, 2) National Radio Astronomy Observatory, and 3) National Aeronautics and Space Administration—and facilities in the U.S., Spain, and Australia. It had a window of opportunity when the relevant planets would be in proper juxtaposition, which required *performance to schedule.* The mission has been a major success to date and is expected to continue to return valuable data well into the twenty-first century, as it speeds out of the sun's magnetic influence and into interstellar space (Bartos and Brundage 1989).

On 11 May 1990, a *$70 million tin-concentrator plant* was dedicated in Portugal for Sociedade Mineira de Neves-Corvo. It was completed $4 million under budget and three months ahead of the fifteen-month schedule. This was "a remarkable achievement considering the tight schedule, complexity of the flow sheets, that equipment and material were imported from 13 countries on four continents, and that only 5 percent of engineering had been completed before construction started" (Bubna and Anderson 1992).

In South Africa, *Sasol,* a South African Petro Chemical Company, began production of a polypropylene facility in February 1990, just twenty-two months after commissioning the R541.7 million project. The completed facility was designed to produce 120,000 ton/annum of polypropylene, fed by a 150,000 ton/annum polymer-grade propylene plant. Previously, the best schedule record for a facility of comparable capacities was thirty months. This outstanding performance "resulted from breaking new ground in project execution methods that will definitely influence the handling of future major projects" (van Zyl 1991).

The economic benefits of this project include employment for 250 people and "a massive R200 million/year savings in foreign currency for South Africa." In addition to realizing these savings as much as eight months early, the early completion enabled Sasol to reach the market sooner and enhance its market share.

AT&T Business Communications Division has equipped all of its project managers with laptop computers with a standard package of software including a critical path method-based project planning and scheduling program. To ensure that project managers are competent in the other 90-plus percent of project management knowledge and skills, the company adopted PMI's project management professional (PMP®) certification program. Other companies have adopted this program as a strategic thrust to assure clients of the competency of their project managers. At least one organization has established PMP certification of project managers as a requirement for bidding on its projects (Ono 1990).

Regardless of the fact that the merger did not last, project management was used to facilitate all of the changes required in preparation for the formal merger of AT&T and NCR. The very large number of decisions and tasks necessary for such an undertaking were accomplished in just ninety days, and they were done so well that customers were not inconvenienced as a result of the merger (Hofstadter 1992).

Xerox Corporation's USA Customer Operations-Information Management organization implemented an enterprisewide project management capability to plan, track, manage, and evaluate all of its projects and resources. This resulted in a 10 percent productivity improvement through reduced training time for employees, reduced time to develop plans for new projects, reduced time to replan, and improved ability to react to deviations from plan (Dalal et al. 1993). Indeed, one of the first requirements to move from level one to level two in the software process maturity framework is to install project management (Zells 1993). This has proven to be beneficial in ensuring that all participants in a project are working toward the same objectives, and that no work that is not a part of approved project plans is going forward in the organization.

The experience of *Syntellect Inc.*, a high-growth computer-system manufacturer of some two hundred personnel, which embarked on a combined strategic planning and total quality-management implementation project, reinforces this notion. The company soon recognized that to ensure focused attention on and meet the target dates for this high-priority project, it was necessary to use the MPM approach. From this experience, the company learned that "success of a strategic plan is far less dependent upon brainstorming and the development of 'killer' ideas than it is upon diligent project management of the very essential but often very ordinary ideas that emerge from the planning process" (Sparks 1993).

The *Bad Creek-pumped storage hydro station by Duke Power* illustrates a major aspect of project management with outstanding logistics management. The dynamos/turbines are located in a cavern carved out of solid rock. There was no room in the cavern for excess materials. Thus, a system was established to move materials to the work site each day, as required by the work to be done the next day. A strong effort was made to ensure that the skilled craftspersons would not be delayed by lack of materials or tools, or have to spend time searching for or checking required materials or tools. In addition, this was an outstanding project in that the entire team was kept informed of progress and celebrated the milestones as they were achieved (Snyder and Caligan 1990).

While most of the projects mentioned are large, complex, and technologically demanding, the same benefits can be achieved on much smaller, less demanding projects. Indeed, many organizations could achieve significant benefits by managing all change efforts using a project-oriented planning, scheduling, and controlling system. Such an effort was undertaken at the Chrysler Corporation's Detroit Universal plant in the sixties, using software that was primitive by today's standards. As a result, projects as simple as writing a new job description to profit improvement projects with high corporate visibility were completed on schedule, a substantial improvement over previous years. These benefits occurred primarily as a result of improved scheduling and utilizing the varied resources within the plant.

The benefits are clear: MPM, wedded to total quality management, can save time and budget, improve implementation of strategic plans, and increase the competitiveness of all sorts of organizations.

Do not expect these benefits to be without cost. In a study published in *The Benefits of Project Management*, it was found that the average cost of project management services as a percentage of project ... spending was 6 percent (Ibbs and Kwak 1997). For the companies participating in the study, this cost ranged from as low as 0.3 percent to as high as 15 percent. The study did not provide a definitive return on investment for these expenditures, primarily due to the differing degrees of implementation of project management across the organizations. A project management maturity model was developed for the study, which did provide some very convincing evidence, albeit preliminary due to the relatively small sample size.

Two measures of project performance were used: a cost index and a schedule index. The cost index was simply the actual project costs divided by the authorized budget. The schedule index was the actual project duration divided by the authorized project duration. For each index, the project performance improved as the level of maturity of project management practices increased. Thus, while benefits of MPM may not be immediately realized, they appear to be substantial, as both experience and degree of application increase.

Another observation in this study is that the 6 percent cost for project management services has been increasing over time. This could be interpreted that organizations have found the application of MPM to be beneficial, for they have continued to increase their funding for it.

CONCLUSION

Projects fill an essential need of society. Indeed, projects constitute the major mode in which change is accomplished in a society. It is also the mode in which corporate strategy is implemented. Projects need be neither large, high tech, nor complex. Their management is often complex, due to the need to closely coordinate a wide variety of resources in a manner to efficiently and effectively achieve the objectives of the project. This is compounded further by the fact that the mix of resources/technologies/operations is constantly changing over the life of the project. And this must be accomplished by doing the right thing right the first time, often with a completely new set of players.

MPM is critical to the future of project-oriented industries/organizations as they strive to match the performance of the volume manufacturing organizations in achieving quality and reliability levels, for which defects are measured in parts per million. It is critical to all organizations that hope to survive in a world where change is occurring at an increasing pace. Projects are the means for responding to, if not proactively anticipating, the environment and opportunities of the future. To delay implementing MPM is akin to taking a rest in the midst of a heated competition: the aggressive leaders will most certainly move ahead.

Chapter II

So What Is a Project?

Several Centuries Later

Help Wanted: Person needed to manage projects. No experience necessary. PM software on hand with instruction manual for its use. You will be responsible for planning, scheduling and controlling all projects done by this organization. Salary negotiable.

OC: Congratulations, Sam, you got the job. You learned in high school that the disk goes in that little slot on the front of the computer box—slide end first and circular metal plate down. You found the switch on the back of the box and ZAP—the computer is working, the software is loaded, and you are ready to manage your first project.

OC: What's that you say? No one told you what to do? That's easy! Just ask one of the old-timers, right? Right!

Sam: Hey, Joe, where's my first project?

OC: Just a word of advice, Sam. Be careful what Old Joe says next. He's a real sport. He's been known to send unsuspecting greenhorns looking for an oven wrench, a sky-hook, or even a left-handed monkey wrench. One morning, he even bothered to bring a gunnysack to work just so he could take this young kid snipe hunting after work. It must have been a great night for hunting 'cause that youngster came draggin' in the next morning lookin' like he'd been up all night. Old Joe came in fit as a fiddle saying something like,

"Gee, these young kids sure don't have much stamina nowadays, do they?" Well, maybe Old Joe's age is softening him up a bit. All he said was:

Joe: "Gee, Sam, I don't know. Hey, Clyde, didn't we have one of them there projects around here a year or two ago?

And so goes the first day on the job. Is this a joke? Well, maybe not as much as it seems. This Olde Curmudgeon has certainly witnessed similar behaviors and may have engaged in one or two. It appears that there will be a lot of Sams out there in the next few years. Consider the following facts and predictions. Sales of project management software have increased substantially in recent years. PMI® membership is growing—fast. A lot of people are using project management software for the first time. Some of them may not be able to recognize a project. Many don't even know they do projects.

A Guide to the Project Management Body of Knowledge (PMBOK® Guide) defines a project as "a temporary endeavor undertaken to create a unique product or service" (1996).

The notion of a temporary process implies uniqueness of the effort, even though it may be composed of operations that are done frequently within the larger organization. The specific arrangement of the operations is not likely to be the same on every project.

One of the most difficult concepts to grasp, it seems, is the difference between the project and the product of the project. For example, a house is built via a project; the house is the product of the project. It is intended to have an extended life. The project is the process by which the house is built, and that process has a finite life that ends when the house is completed. The start of this project may be defined differently, depending on the scope of the project; i.e., it could range from the recognition of a need for a house to signing a contract with a builder.

A project proceeds by a process of progressive elaboration. A project, in the broadest context, is initiated by a person who recognizes a problem or an opportunity for which some action is to be taken. That person, alone or in concert with others, develops an initial concept of a product—a new facility, an advertising campaign, or the like. Much work needs to be accomplished to take this meager concept to

16

the reality of the product of the project. The general concept is expanded into a more detailed statement of requirements. This is examined for feasibility—market, technical, legal, organizational, political, and the like—resulting in further refinement of the specifications. These become the basis for general design, the products of which are the specifications for detail design. The detail designs are followed by production designs—tooling, production instructions, and so forth—and each stage produces an elaboration on the specifications of the prior stage.

Eventually, the product of the project takes shape, is tested, and is ready for operation or sale. At this stage, give or take a few details, the project is completed.

Having stripped away the unnecessary, it is clear that a project is a process. The essential concept of this process is that it is the progressive elaboration of requirements/specifications.

From this, it is easy to integrate the essential concepts of modern quality management, including "conformance to requirements/specifications," "the customer is the next person/operation in the process," "do the right thing right the first time," and, ultimately, "statistical process control."

A TAXONOMY OF WORK EFFORTS

It can be argued that a project is a project because I choose to define it as a project and manage it as a project. This sounds like heresy, but the more complex projects are done using several modes of organizing the work effort. Understanding the alternative modes will aid in gaining a clear concept of a project.

There are five basic modes in which work is accomplished: 1) craft, 2) project, 3) job shop, 4) progressive line, and 5) continuous flow. While most organizations perform some work in several of these modes, generally one mode is dominant in the core technology of the organization. For example, some organizations are inherently project oriented—such as construction companies, research labs, movie production, theater, and, yes, even political campaigns.

All of these modes can be characterized as processes composed of one or more technologies/operations. Technologies in this sense do not imply only engineering or manufacturing technologies, but include all sorts of office technologies—the copier as well as the computer—and the *technologies* involved in producing an advertising or political campaign, designing a training program or curriculum, or producing a movie. Consider the following definitions and discussions of the five modes.

1. **Craft**: a process composed of a collection of one or more technologies/operations involving homogeneous human resources, generally a single person, producing a narrow range of products/services.

This mode is best characterized by the single artist/craftsman producing one unit of product at a time. Examples include a single cook preparing a meal to order or a doctor examining a patient in the doctor's office. In a project, there are often tasks that are performed in the craft mode—one person doing the entire task. One backhoe/front-loader operator may well excavate a site for a small building, such as a house; one carpenter may notch and trim the roof joists for a house. One person often writes computer programs, and certainly one person frequently performs software maintenance and modification. All of these are examples from what might be a project in its entirety, but the specific task is done in craft mode.

2. **Project**: a temporary process (composed of a loosely coordinated collection of heterogeneous technologies/operations) undertaken to create one or a few units of a unique product or service for which specifications are progressively elaborated.

A popular myth is that only defense, space, construction, and other large endeavors are projects. Projects come in all sizes, industries, functions, and degrees of complexity. Purchasing and installing a home entertainment center may well be a project. Major surgery is generally done in project mode. Most change efforts in a society are performed in project mode. Some endeavors are composed of several to many interrelated projects, in which case they may be referred to as a program.

3. **Job shop**: a process composed of a loosely coordinated collection of heterogeneous technologies/operations to create a wide range of products/services, where the technologies are located in groups by function, and the time required at each workstation is varied.

This mode is best characterized by the manufacturing plant in which equipment is located or grouped into departments by type or function, and the operations are performed by moving the unit being worked upon from one department to another.

This is the mode of operation used by most commercial kitchens and is typically used for physical examinations performed in hospitals. The job-shop mode is frequently used on projects to reduce the cost of components. For example, for a development composed of a large number of houses, a job shop might be set up to precut much of the lumber and assemble sections of partitions using jigs to hold the studs and plates in place while nailing them together. A major building may be designed using a repetitive precast concrete panel for exterior facing. Manufacturing the panels in job-shop mode could result in substantial cost savings.

The prototype parts for a new helicopter project are produced in a job shop producing one or a few units of each part. Looking at only one part going through this job shop, it can appear deceptively like a project. But when the shop is viewed as a whole, it becomes readily apparent that the parts are only a few of the many going through that same shop. On even closer examination it is easy to see that the dependency relationship between parts in the system is very loose if it exists at all. On the other hand, it is quite conceivable that the same shop could get a very large contract for a prototype assembly and would choose to manage it in the project mode.

Thus, to an extent, a project is a project because we choose to manage it as a project.

4. **Progressive line**: a process composed of a serially located collection of heterogeneous technologies/operations to produce a large quantity of a limited range of products/services. The operator is directly involved in the work on the product, and the time allotted at each workstation is nearly the same.

The automotive assembly line is the stereotypical example, with the product moving from station to station in a cycle time of approximately sixty seconds. Since this mode is used for both assembly and disassembly, the general term *progressive line* is more appropriate. Progressive line is also the typical mode of serving in cafeterias and the mode in which physical examinations are given to large groups of people, such as for the military.

Progressive-line mode may be used within a project. One example is a project to construct 740 houses in a development. The houses were in fact erected in the progressive-line mode with multiple crews, each crew performing a very specific task on each house. On this line, the crews moved from house to house with a cycle time of approximately one day.

Close examination reveals that this is the dominant mode for erection of a large office or manufacturing building. One team sets the structural steel in place. Other teams come along sequentially to secure the bolts or rivets, construct the forms, install reinforcing, pour the concrete, and yet another removes the forms. When well planned, each team takes the same amount of time to perform its task, and the teams just keep moving from floor to floor or bay to bay.

It is very likely that a many-paged report will be assembled in progressive-line mode with piles of each sheet stacked around a table and the people walking around the table picking a sheet from each stack, except when those sheets come off of a modern-day copier with a collator. Then the process is essentially in the continuous-flow mode.

5. **Continuous flow**: a process composed of a serially located collection of technologies/operations that is applied uniformly over time to all the many units of a very narrow range of products/services, and in which the role of the operator is primarily to monitor and adjust the processes.

Petroleum refineries are the most popular example of this mode. In addition, based on an examination of the characteristics of this mode, electric generating stations; water, as well as sewage treatment facilities; and automatic transfer lines such as those used in producing engine blocks and transmission housings are examples of this mode. It is often used in projects to get the cost as low as possible or sometimes due to a technological requirement. For example, not only is concrete pouring by a pumper truck more economical, but also on large pours it may almost be a necessity to achieve a continuous bonding of the poured concrete. Examples of this are highways and the massive cooling towers often found at electrical generating stations.

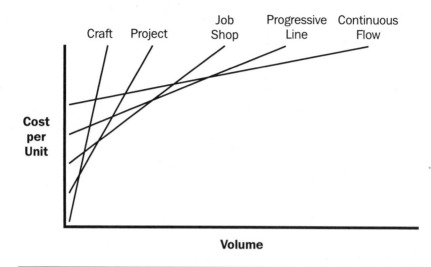

FIGURE II.1

Cost-Volume Break-Even Curves for Alternative Modes of Work

Understanding the economics of these modes, as shown in Figure II.1, reveals a fundamental driving force for attempting to move from craft mode as far as possible toward continuous-flow mode. For a given type of work, the craft mode generally requires the least capital investment or fixed costs but the highest variable cost per unit, while continuous mode requires large capital investments or fixed costs and very low variable costs per unit. The other modes tend to be arrayed between these two extremes. Thus, regardless of the major mode for a given undertaking, there should always be a search for subsets of the work to be moved to the more economical mode.

This was done, for example, for the eighty thousand seats in the Pontiac (Michigan) Silverdome stadium, which were installed in the progressive-line mode. Perhaps the most impressive application of progressive-line manufacturing on a project was on the Northumberland Crossing Bridge construction. Two lines were set up, one to fabricate the concrete piers and the other to fabricate the concrete box-beam spans. The piers consisted of two conical-shaped components, one of which rested on the ocean floor and the other on top of it. They were designed to resist the forces of ice flows in the winter and, indeed, break up ice that jammed behind them. The other line, for the box-beam spans, produced components longer than a football field. When they were completed, they were moved to the end of a causeway, where they were then transferred to a barge that resembled a giant forklift that carried them to the position where they were set upon a pier and joined to the previously installed span. On the ground, both pier and span sections were moved from station to station on a very large tracked vehicle similar to the one used at Cape Kennedy to transport space-shuttle assemblies from the assembly building to the launch platform.

This was also done in the English Channel Tunnel project, where the digging, moving of tailings, and pumping of slurry to the tailings pit were all done in the continuous-flow mode. In fact, all modes can be observed on that project. This same phenomenon can be seen in many much simpler and smaller projects.

Thus, projects are an essential method of accomplishing the work of society. They are the means by which change is accomplished, including but not limited to the development of new products, creation of new facilities, designing a new curriculum, and many other such endeavors. However, the project manager must be knowledgeable of the other modes in which work is performed in order to complete the project within the optimum cost and schedule.

THE NATURE OF PROJECTS

Projects come in all sorts of shapes, sizes, and degrees of complexity. That is what makes them such a challenge.

Projects can be very small. The concepts have been used to considerable advantage for planning a small weekend family project, clarifying such things as:
❑ identifying all the tasks that must be done
❑ understanding the sequence in which these tasks need to be done
❑ understanding which tasks could be performed by which members of the family

❏ identifying required tools and materials, so they can all be obtained in one trip to the store
❏ recognizing which activities could be performed indoors in the event of rain
❏ achieving agreement with the plan from the spouse and other family members
❏ convincing the spouse that the *simple, little* project is neither as simple nor as little as imagined.

These same benefits were achieved in building a house, resulting in considerable savings compared to what the cost would have been without such careful planning. A review of the projects cited in the previous chapter illustrate the size and complexity of projects and how modern project management has resulted in savings of both time and cost on them.

Life Cycles

Another way to distinguish projects from the product of projects is to compare the life cycles of a set of related projects and products. For example, suppose that it is decided to develop a new product. The product typically has a life cycle composed of introduction, growth, maturity, and decline phases, as seen in Figure II.2, The Relationship between Product and Project Life Cycles.

Initiating a product development project develops the product. It might have a life cycle composed of basic research, product research, product design, and production phases. Notice that the marketing life cycle does not begin until the product life cycle reaches the production phase.

The product is produced in a capital facility that must be created. This facility has a life cycle that might include feasibility, acquisition, operations and maintenance, and disposal. Note that the production phase of the product cycle cannot start until the capital facility is in the operations and maintenance phase.

The facility is created by a project that might have the following phases: conceptual, development, implementation, and termination. The conceptual and development phases of the project are probably

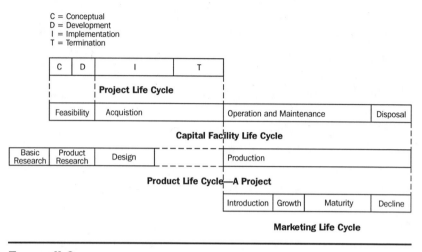

C = Conceptual
D = Development
I = Implementation
T = Termination

FIGURE II.2

Relationship Between Product and Project Life Cycles

concurrent with the feasibility phase for the facility, while the implementation and termination phases for the project are concurrent with the acquisition phase of the facility. Although not shown in Figure II.2, there are likely to be additional projects associated with the maintenance of the facility, increasing the capacity of the facility and the changes in marketing approaches for the product as it moves from one phase to the next.

"The ... project life cycles [shown in Figures II-3–II-6] have been chosen to illustrate the diversity of approaches in use. The examples shown are typical; they are neither recommended nor preferred. In each case, the phase names and major deliverables are those described by the author" (*PMBOK® Guide*).

The *PMBOK® Guide* provides very good examples of the phases used in different industries.

Projects have a characteristic curve of the use of resources over their life cycles, as shown in Figure II.7. During the conceptual phase, there are generally relatively few resources involved as decisions are made about the scope of the product, as well as the scope of the project. During the development phase, resource usage grows some-

"**Defense acquisition.** The US Department of Defense directive 5000.2, as revised February 1993, describes a series of acquisition milestones and phases as illustrated in" Figure II.3.

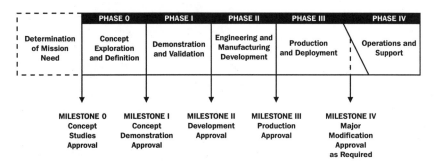

Source: *A Guide to the Project Management Body of Knowledge* (*PMBOK® Guide*), PMI Standards Committee, 1996.

FIGURE II.3

Representative Life Cycle for Defense Acquisition, per US DOD 5000.2 (Rev. 2/26/93)

what. Resource usage is typically highest during the implementation phase, decreasing after the bulk of that effort is completed. The number of resources required decreases even further during the termination phase.

This phenomenon can be plotted as illustrated in Figure II.8, as a cumulative curve that resembles an "S"; therefore, it is called the "S" curve of projects.

SUMMARY

It is an interesting anomaly that all people have performed a variety of projects. It is somewhat like learning to walk or speak. Certainly, projects have been used throughout the ages to accomplish many of the needs of society. However, in the last fifty years, we have learned a great deal more about the nature of projects and how they differ from other modes of work efforts. The knowledge has been converted from

"**Construction**. Morris [1] describes a construction project life cycle as illustrated in" Figure II.4. A go/no-go decision is made at the end of the feasibility phase. Major contracts have been let by the end of the planning and design phase. The facility is substantially completed by the end of the production phase and is fully operable by the end of this phase.

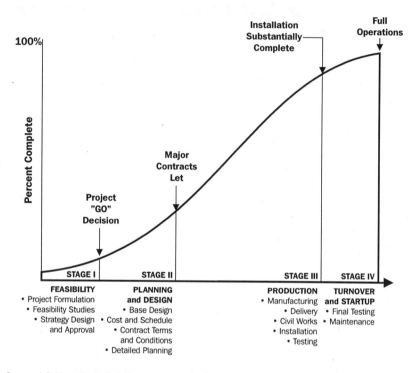

Source: *A Guide to the Project Management Body of Knowledge* (*PMBOK® Guide*), PMI Standards Committee, 1996.

FIGURE II.4

Representative Constructive Project Life Cycle, per Morris

conventional wisdom to precise concepts and tools that enable projects to be performed more efficiently and effectively. It has been difficult to codify all this knowledge, as projects have such great variety. However, one of the precepts of PMI is that there is an extensive body of knowledge common to all projects. There are excellent opportunities to learn how your projects can be performed better by observing

"**Pharmaceuticals**. Murphy [2] describes a project life cycle for pharmaceutical new product development in the United States as illustrated in" Figure II.5. The diagram is of a summary project network diagram with the phases shown below.

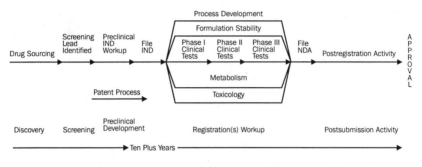

Source: *A Guide to the Project Management Body of Knowledge (PMBOK® Guide)*, PMI Standards Committee, 1996.

FIGURE II.5

Representative Life Cycle for a Pharmaceuticals Project, per Murphy

and listening to how others have performed their projects—even though they seem quite different.

Sam had learned that projects come in all forms, shapes, and sizes. Some work is clearly best done by projects. Other work is best done in craft, job-shop, progressive-line, or continuous-flow mode. Indeed, some of the work in projects may be accomplished more efficiently, more effectively, or both in one of the other modes. Thus, the project manager must be aware of these possibilities.

Some of the work that has traditionally been done in one of these other modes may now be done more efficiently, more effectively, or both in project mode. Thus, it is important to question old adages such as, "We've always done it this way," and, "We tried that once, and it didn't work." New opportunities are available today as the result of the development of modern project management.

"**Software development**. Muench, et al. [3] describe a model for software development with four cycles and four quadrants as illustrated in" Figure II.6. The cycles correspond to phases.

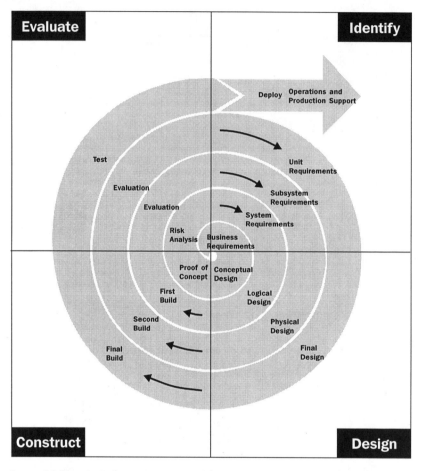

Source: *A Guide to the Project Management Body of Knowledge (PMBOK® Guide)*, PMI Standards Committee, 1996.

FIGURE II.6

Representative Software Development Life Cycle, per Muench

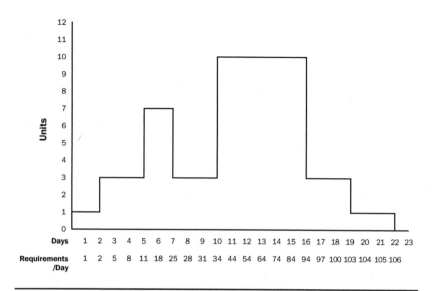

FIGURE II.7

Resource Usage Over the Life Cycle of a Project

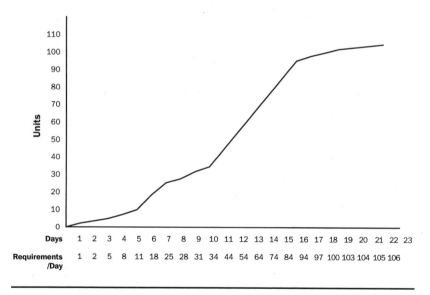

FIGURE II.8

Cumulative Resource Usage Over the Life Cycle of a Project:
The "S" Curve

Chapter III

Modern
Project Management

Sam was overwhelmed. The magnitude of this project was greater than had ever been attempted before. Sam sought the wisdom of the past by trekking to the Cave of the Elders. Fortunately, among all the hieroglyphics, Sam discovered some great wisdom on a large tablet. Sam returned to the riverbank with the tablet, determined to practice these new precepts.

THE DEVELOPMENT OF MODERN PROJECT MANAGEMENT

Managing projects is certainly not a new concept; there is an infinite number of examples of small and great projects through the ages that have been managed—often very effectively. As other aspects of living on Earth have changed over time, the needs and methods for managing projects have changed. In the last half-century, the approaches to managing projects have changed dramatically.

Project management as a unique career and profession is barely forty years old. Its origins can be traced to efforts such as the United States Department of Defense major weapons-systems development, National Aeronautics and Space Administration space missions, and major construction and maintenance efforts, as well as comparable efforts in Europe. The magnitude and complexity of these efforts were the driving force in the search for tools that could aid management in the planning, decision-making, and control of the multitude of activities involved in such projects, especially those with many activities occurring simultaneously.

A major misconception about project management is that it is program evaluation and review technique, critical path method, or project-scheduling software by any other name. A more realistic view is that scheduling software is a small part of project management. Its importance is that it has permitted scheduling and cost management to be done much more efficiently, and therefore either in less time or in more detail—or both. Hence, a project can be planned and executed more precisely and leave more time to perform the other aspects of project management.

An important way to view project management is as the *management of change*. This statement is more meaningful when contrasted with three other types of management: 1) operations, 2) technical, and 3) general.

Operations management can be characterized as *managing the steady state*. A new operation—e.g., a manufacturing facility—is created by a project. It achieves return on investment by continued, repetitive usage, by producing large quantities of a product for sale. This is achieved through operations management, concerned with obtaining output and maintaining the operation in a productive mode for as long as possible. Maximizing the life of the operation often requires maintenance or modifications of the facility that are done as projects. Typically, a project manager manages these projects separately from the ongoing operation.

Technical management tends to focus on theory, technology, and practice in a technical field, concerning itself with questions of policy on strength of materials, design methodology, safety factors in design, checking procedures, and the like. The products of technical management are typically designs of products to be produced in volume or designs of the facilities in which these products are to be produced. Technical operations have often been managed as job shops, with emphasis on efficient use of resources as measured by the number of drawings produced per time period. Some engineering jobs are sufficiently important to manage as projects, with more emphasis on early completion than on efficiency.

General management has responsibility for the organization as a whole. These executives concern themselves with organizational policy and strategy. Strategy involves change, which is accomplished via projects. Executives tend to be concerned about setting up new operations (via projects) to implement organizational strategy. As soon as the operation is established, the concern is more with maintaining the operation in a productive mode, i.e., operations management.

Modern project management (MPM) is the interface between operations, technical, and general management, integrating all aspects of the project and causing the project to happen. Software provides considerable assistance by identifying those activities that must be performed in a time period, the number of units of resource required by day for a given schedule, and the activities on which a critical resource is required. Nevertheless, having identified the critical decision areas, human judgment is still required to evaluate and make the final decisions.

One of the essential concepts of MPM is the assigning of a single person as the project manager for the project. In the past, responsibility for total project management was often diffused. This could be explained by several motivations. It may have been a way for some executives to avoid giving up power. It may have been a way of spreading responsibility or blame. It may have been because the executive assigned responsibility for managing the project could not possibly spend the time necessary to manage it effectively and so, by default, allowed others to exercise responsibility. Often this spreading of responsibility was *justified* by the desire to have everyone who was concerned about the project to be involved. Whatever the motivations, projects were often completed late, overran budgets, achieved less than expected, and sometimes led to disasters for themselves, the responsible person, and/or the organization. Often this was a result of untimely or ill-informed decisions. Contractors and vendors had difficulty identifying to whom they should take their problems, leading to the use of strategies that would get the most favorable decision for them rather than for the project.

Gradually, it was recognized that assigning a single person as project manager with adequate time to do the job well solved many of the problems, including those cited earlier. As this happened, the more aggressive project managers started realizing that they needed more skills and knowledge than they had garnered to date, so they looked for others with similar experience to share their concerns and seek guidance. It was in an effort to fulfill this need that organizations such as the Project Management Institute (PMI®) were born.

Another feature of MPM is the focus on developing a common language for all activities on the project. This was made vivid to the OC when, upon implementation of a new project management system for the construction of an automotive assembly plant, the vice president of car assembly stated, "At last, our engineers, accountants, and construction people can all talk the same language." If the import of this comment is not obvious to the reader, at that time it was common practice for each of these disciplines, and others, to present information in the format most convenient to its practitioners. The responsible executive was required to guess the correlation between the amount spent on each item, what physical progress had actually been made, and what it all implied about the future of the project. (There will be more on this subject in a chapter on cost management in *PM 102*.)

There are more observations about the features of MPM in the rest of this chapter. They include significant improvements in schedule and cost control, resource management, progress and status reporting and forecasting, and the ability to manage change appropriately and avoid disputes.

DIMENSIONS OF PROJECT MANAGEMENT

There are three dimensions of managing a project that need clarification before proceeding: 1) technical, 2) leadership, and 3) administrative.

Technical

Project management is typically thought of in terms of management of the technical issues associated with a project. This is not unreasonable, for a common title for the person who seemed to be managing a construction project in the past has been *project engineer*. Computer-systems projects have often been managed by a *lead systems analyst*. Similarly, across the range of types of projects, the apparent manager of the project has been a senior technical person. Often this person reported to a senior manager, who gave some attention to a variety of projects, but also had significant responsibilities for an ongoing operation. Typically this would be someone such as the vice president of manufacturing for a plant project or the director of management information systems for computer-related projects. With attention divided between operating responsibilities and several projects, the attention to the project was often *review* in nature as opposed to proactive management. Similarly, the senior technical person was often drawn into the technical issues to an extent that precluded actual *managing* of the project. Thus, the orderly flow of work for all of the activities in the project was often left to the good intentions of the participants.

Perhaps an example will illustrate this best. The OC observed rather closely the construction of a fifteen thousand-seat arena. The construction superintendent was on the job in the field and ostensibly responsible for the efficient construction of the building. Things were moving along well until the structural steel began arriving. Soon it was noticed that the first steel to arrive was for the upper stories; no one had directed the steel fabricator to deliver the first-story steel first. (It fabricated steel in the sequence it received drawings.) As corporate executives began to realize that construction was grinding to a halt, they dispatched a senior manager to solve the problem. In a private conversation, he admitted that no one back at the home office or at the construction site had been assigned total responsibility for the expeditious construction of the building. It was discovered that the problem was really a conflict between the structural engineering design firm and the firm hired to do the detail fabrication drawings. The costs of having a project manager for this job would have been more than recouped by avoiding the excess costs arising from the structural steel problems.

There were other ramifications of the absence of a project manager. A one hundred-plus-ton crane had been brought to the job site shortly before structural steel erection was to begin. It sat idle with its boom resting on the ground for several months while the steel-delivery sequence problem was being resolved. Also, no one was really paying attention to quality control on the steel. As a result, several steel columns were mismarked and installed in the wrong location. Considerable expense was incurred in rework to move the pieces to their proper locations. The same crane that had been idle was occupied with holding up the steel supported by these columns while the rework was going on.

Time after time, the OC has observed projects that have been the responsibility of someone who had full-time responsibility for an ongoing operation. Seldom have these projects been executed in anywhere near an efficient manner. On the other hand, projects with full-time, competent project managers have generally been brought in on or better than schedule and budget.

None of the above is to denigrate the technical aspects of the project. If they are not performed in a competent manner, the project is not likely to be a success. However, we need to understand the nature of the technical activities, and recognize which are the project manager's responsibility and which belong to the technical representative on the project team. On any project, there are technical issues that require work and decisions; some have to do with overall concepts of the product of the project. This might be site and plant layout for the construction project or the overall systems design for a computer systems project. These should be the primary responsibility of the technical person, but the project manager should be involved. There are detail drawings for the construction project or module design for the computer project; the project manager should not be involved in most of these except to monitor their timely performance.

There is another class of design problem that is often not well understood: systems engineering. If the project manager truly has a technical responsibility, this is the primary one. Consider a simple project: the design of a home entertainment system. Just a cursory knowledge of audio/video systems leads to awareness that the best performance for the money is a balanced system. The best tuner in the world will not realize its potential if the speakers are inadequate to produce the sound received from the tuner. It would be better to balance the expenditures on these two components to achieve optimum performance of the system. Now, when we consider all of the components of the home entertainment center, the magnitude and importance of this problem becomes apparent. The project manager should be quite aware of, if not involved in, these system tradeoffs.

The essence of this problem is well described by the mathematics of the reliability model. Given "n" components in a system with equal probability of failure, the probability of the system failing is:

$$\text{Pr}_{\text{system}} = 1 - (1 - \text{Pr}_{\text{component}})^n$$

where: $\text{Pr}_{\text{system}}$ = probability of system failure

$\text{Pr}_{\text{component}}$ = probability of component failure

n = the number of components

If the probability of failure of the components is the same—say, .01— the probability of system failure with increasing numbers of components is shown in column 2 of Table III.1.

If the probabilities of the components are unequal this simply becomes:

$$\text{Pr}_{\text{system}} = 1 - (1 - \text{Pr}_{\text{component 1}})(1 - \text{Pr}_{\text{component 2}})(\text{Pr}_{\text{component 3}}), \text{ etc.}$$

or

$$= 1 - \pi_{i=1}^{n} (1 - \text{Pr}_{\text{component } i})$$

If the component failure probabilities are unequal—i.e., unbalanced—the probability of system failure increases appreciably as a function of the degree of imbalance, as shown in columns 3 and 4 of Table III.1. This is analogous to the performance of a system by most any measure.

COLUMN 1	COLUMN 2	COLUMN 3	COLUMN 4
Number of Components	Equal Probabilities	One at .005 Rest at .02	One at .001 Rest at .03
1	.0100	—	—
2	.0199	.0249	.0310
3	.0297	.0444	.0600
4	.0394	.0635	.0882
5	.0490	.0822	.1156

TABLE III.1

Probabilities of System Failure as a Function of Component Failure Probabilities

If the project manager is going to be involved in the technical aspects of the project, this is the level that is most applicable. If the project is large, it may require the full-time attention of a systems engineer.

The other side of the coin is that for the first project to which the aspiring project manager is assigned, the technical aspects of the project may well be her total responsibility. Thus, such a person must be competent at some level in all three dimensions: 1) technical, 2) leadership, and 3) administrative.

Leadership

Even had there been a project manager on the earlier-mentioned arena project, it is likely that its problem would not have been avoided if the project manager lacked leadership skills necessary to become aware of the problem, determine appropriate action, convince others that action is necessary, and cause action to be taken. Thus, while it could be considered an intangible skill, the results of leadership are clearly discernible throughout the smooth performance of the project. Without adequate time to perform the tasks necessary to exercise that leadership, it is not likely to happen. All too often, people with responsibility behave as bureaucratic persons and leave the real problem to someone else to solve.

Bureaucratic Man—behaves in such a way as to minimize problems to himself.

Administrative

The administrative aspects of a project are often the most neglected. Even when corporate policies and procedures prescribe administrative requirements, they often get lower priority than the technical aspects of the project. It is questionable if an organization's personal-expense reimbursement procedure would be followed expeditiously if it did not mean money in the individual's pocket. It is possible that there was a corporate policy or procedure that dealt with the scheduling of components going into the arena that should have prevented the structural steel problems in the aforementioned arena construction, but, if so, it was not followed.

Previous to the modern project scheduling tools, rescheduling was something that was done only when deviation from schedule was so bad that no one knew the status of the project. Today, this method is totally unsatisfactory. Someone has to monitor schedule performance, try to keep the project on schedule, and reschedule activities that are impractical or perhaps impossible to accomplish according to the existing schedule. Cost management in the past was much the same with most cost control performed through a very limited number of work orders. The ability to correlate physical progress with actual expenditures was severely limited.

Thus, MPM emphasizes project performance in many respects—schedule, cost, quality, public acceptance, and so on—that were not given adequate attention in the past.

ASSIGNING RESPONSIBILITIES

The project manager's major responsibility is to manage the project and the project team. The degree of authority that is granted to a specific project manager is dependent upon the individual, the project, the organization, and the client.

The Individual

The most important factor is the confidence that the organization has in the individual, and the most direct contributor to this is that individual's past experience. Clearly, successful performance of a series of progressively larger projects promotes confidence in an individual. Performance of a similar project is even better. Demonstrated leadership skills are a must. They can be demonstrated as an employee on projects within the organization, as an employee of another organization, or even as a volunteer leader on significant company or community projects. The OC gained considerable experience and confidence of management as program manager for meetings of the Chrysler headquarters management club. The opportunities are readily available; they are most effective if they are in an area valued by the top management of the organization.

Size of the Project

You become a project manager one zero at a time. Clearly, your first project will not likely be one with many zeros, whether measured in dollars, labor hours, or whatever. It is important to recognize each project assignment as an opportunity to create confidence in your ability to handle more responsibility. Most people, most of the time, will advance one zero at a time. Outstanding performance often leads to advancing two or more zeros at a time. Except for very unusual circumstances, failure on a project will result in falling back one or more zeros, and it will require exceptional performance to get on the *fast track*. Thus, excellent performance on each assignment is very important.

Importance of the Project to the Organization

Sometimes a project will be so important that it has the potential to destroy the organization if it is not successful. An example would be the development of a replacement for the major product of an organization or the merger of two large organizations. The CEO is most likely to be the project manager. Another example is a major operating millage campaign for a public school system. In this case, the superintendent of schools will likely be the *de facto* project manager. While you may be the project manager in name on such a project, you are truly the assistant project manager. In most respects, you should behave as the project manager, but maintain a much closer liaison with the CEO. The same phenomenon occurs for divisions of an organization; the head of the division will be deeply involved in a project that is critical to that division.

The Desires of the Client

The client of the project can have a great deal to do with who becomes the project manager. On a project to computerize five control loops of a cupola in a major cast-iron foundry, the contract specifically required that the person who made the sales presentation, or an alternative acceptable to the client, would be project manager for the vendor. That led to some heartache on the part of the vendor but was finally accepted. This state-of-the-art project was successfully accomplished within acceptable schedule and budget targets.

Matching the Individual to the Project

One path leading to managing large projects is to start by managing small projects. Another approach is to be assigned less responsibility for a larger project. There are alternatives for matching the responsibilities and authority of the individual to the project including titles such as project expediter, project coordinator, project manager in a matrixed organization, and project manager of a projectized project. When thinking about these, it is best to consider them as points on a continuum of increasing responsibilities and authority with an infinite number of variations based on specific responsibilities and authority. They are discussed briefly to introduce the concepts, relying on the reader to seek other sources for a more thorough discussion.

41

Project expediter is the lowest level of responsibility, assisting in the development of the schedule and budget, gathering information on performance and problems, informing the person who is acting as project manager, as well as others involved on the project. This might be an excellent opportunity for a recent graduate who seems to have potential but little or no experience. She could perform in this role on a project that is much larger than she is prepared to manage.

Project coordinator is the next range on the continuum with, for example, additional responsibilities for conducting meetings on schedule and budget. He might be given authority to authorize overtime within some prescribed limits. The manner in which the person responsible for the project directs others to *cooperate* with this individual can lead to him having *de facto* authority, exceeding his formal authority. Leadership skills will enhance this authority. If these responsibilities are performed well, this position can lead to increased confidence in the individual's capabilities that will in turn lead to greater responsibilities.

In a **matrixed organization**, the project manager is assigned greater responsibilities for schedule and budget. To be most effective, this individual should have the authority to release budget for performance of the work packages. This is one of the most effective means of ensuring the cooperation of functional managers with the project manager. The project manager may well have a project team of key individuals, depending on the size and importance of the project. While many projects of this type are performed without co-location of the key team members, co-location is a major contributor to the expeditious performance of the project. Other team members will probably remain in, and be under the direction of, their respective functional organizations.

Depending on the degree to which the organization is committed to the matrix concept, there may be a manager of project managers. This person must perform as a mentor, troubleshooter, and advocate; he would generally have a higher level of authority, such as ability to commit the organization, that is greater than the project manager's authority.

The project manager on a **projectized project** typically has most of the key team members reporting directly. Yet, it must be remembered that each team member has a function to which she expects to return or upon which she will be dependent for her next assignment after the completion of the project. The determination as to whether the team member will report to the project manager will be based on the amount of work and for what period that type of work will be required on the project. On extremely large projects, even the project manager may change, due to the nature of the capabilities required in various phases of the project.

Again, the specific responsibilities and authorities associated with each of these job titles vary greatly. It is through these variations that the organization can exercise control over the individual, and ensure development of individuals who can assume greater responsibilities in the future.

Executives should recognize that they may have a tendency to hold too much authority to themselves and, due to their other responsibilities, become the bottleneck for the project.

MANAGING THE MILIEU OF THE PROJECT

What does the project manager actually manage? Simply, there are four aspects of the project that need to be recognized as being in need of managing: 1) the project, 2) the project team, 3) the functional managers associated with the project, and 4) the stakeholders.

The Project

The project can be characterized simply in terms of eight concepts: 1) what, 2) why, 3) where, 4) when, 5) who, 6) how, 7) how much, and 8) within what limits.

What is to be done? What is the nature of the product of the project? Is it to last forever or only for a weekend concert? Is it a standard pre-built steel building or a space vehicle?

Why is it needed? Some people, especially some clients, may believe that this is not relevant. However, the more the project manager understands about the need for the product of the project, the better the decisions can be made and the more likely the product will meet the true needs of the client.

Where is the product of the project to be delivered, and where is the project to be performed? While it was the product of a subproject, the major processing plant of the Endicott Oil Field project was fabricated on a barge on the Mississippi River and floated all the way to the Arctic shores of Alaska. Some six weeks after it arrived, it started processing hydrocarbons. Thus, where the product is to be delivered and where the project is to be performed are not trivial questions. Consider the degree to which software projects are contracted out to companies all over the world today.

When is the product of the project required? Does the client have specific scheduling requirements? For example, is there an industry trade show at which it is to be introduced as a new product? Is its introduction based on a prototype of the product or the actual products produced by product of the project? Computer companies have been notorious for multiple introductions of the same product.

Who is to perform the project? Are they assigned full time until their responsibilities are completed, or are they assigned part time with other responsibilities that sometimes take precedence over the project? Are they the best people for the job, those that happen to be available at the time, or the ones to whom their functional manager really does not want to assign any other work?

Who is to represent the client? Avoid like the plague having several persons representing the client. You need a single point of contact with enough authority to make, or get, the necessary decisions in a timely manner—you hope. Sometimes the client will want to provide some equipment or material. Sometimes, she will want to select a vendor. Sometimes, she will want to perform some of the work herself. You need a clear line of responsibility within the client's organization.

How is the project to be performed? Must the project be performed under top-secret security conditions (Strategic Defense Initiative, for example)? Specific phase approvals may be required. Specific approval of some vendors or of contracts for major items may be required.

How much is to be done? What are the limits on costs? What are the minimum performance requirements of the product of the project? What requirements must be met in performing the project?

What are the limits? Limits may be as important as requirements. For example, a highway-improvement project may have to be done without hindering the flow of traffic during normal peak traffic hours. It may have to minimize impact on local businesses. A space project must have limits due to the payload capacities and total dependence upon the space vehicle during the mission.

The Project Team

The project team may be considered at three levels: 1) the core team, 2) the extended team, and 3) the total team.

The *core team* includes those who are directly involved on the project. On the small project, they may be spending only a part of their time, but they have clearly defined responsibilities for bringing the project to completion. Generally, a relatively small number of individuals are the key decision-makers. Sometimes the core team will include major contractors and vendors, due to their significance in the success of the project. The project manager must keep them well informed and highly motivated throughout the project.

The *extended team* includes all specifically assigned to the project. Often these individuals remain located in their functional areas, subject to the priorities of their functional management. Thus, the project manager must ensure that the functional managers are informed and adequately motivated to support the project. As the project gets larger, extended team members may be assigned full time to the project. This generally improves the opportunities to motivate these people, but the project manager must be mindful that each individual has to maintain a relationship with his functional manager, upon whom he will be dependent at the conclusion of his tenure on the project.

The *total team* includes all the people in your and the client's organization, who have significant tasks to perform on the project. It includes the contractors and vendors and their personnel who are directly engaged in work on or for the project. While the project manager does not need to be as concerned with motivation of those on the total team (not included above), it is desirable to ensure that they are favorably disposed to the project.

Functional Managers

Although we referred to the functional managers as a part of the extended team, it is important to understand their role in the project to better understand the need to manage their attitudes toward the project. Specifically in the matrix organization, they are responsible for who and how. The functional manager is responsible for ensuring that the organization has competent people to perform the work, and the work is performed in such a manner to ensure that it meets all technical and legal requirements. This will often prove frustrating to the project manager, but should be viewed as the best protection that the project manager has from producing an unsatisfactory product.

Stakeholders

The term *stakeholder* is defined in *A Guide to the Project Management Body of Knowledge* (*PMBOK® Guide*) as "individuals and organizations who are involved in or may be affected by project activities." In the previous discussion, we mentioned the customer/client, the parent management, and contractors/vendors. In addition, the project manager must keep in mind the interests of stockholders of both the parent organization and the client's organization, regulatory agencies, the community, and governments.

Stockholders of the parent organization expect that the project will lead to profitability. The client organization's stockholders will expect that the product of the project will lead to profitability. Stockholders are not likely to be aware of successful small projects; however, word of unsuccessful projects of any size often leaks out.

Regulatory agencies expect the project as well as the product of the project to conform to all relevant regulations. Sometimes, zealous regulators will insist on exercising some control to assert their power. Thus, some might argue it is wise to leave something on which they can *provide guidance.* This is not recommended as normal practice but is rather left to the project manager to consider judiciously.

The *community,* however it is defined for a specific project, may decide to have its say on the project, often with considerable justification. An excellent example is a tunnel on a major interstate going east out of Seattle, Washington. It was originally conceived of as a *cut* at a much lesser cost for both construction and operations. A cut would have literally cut the community into two separate parts. As a result of community pressure, the plans were changed to a tunnel with the surface space above the right-of-way being made into a park to rejoin the two halves of the community—as a part of the project. There are many examples—e.g., nuclear generating stations—that might be cited to illustrate the concerns and involvement of the community. The project manager must be cognizant of potential community concerns and manage the relationship with the community very carefully. Failure to be concerned with these stakeholders can lead to substantial delays and rework costs.

Governments as stakeholders must be considered at two levels: the body and the individuals. As governmental bodies, they are concerned with protecting the interests of their constituents. Keeping them informed and seeking their advice on the legitimate interests of their constituents can create a cooperative attitude of the body. Failure to generate that cooperative attitude can result in individuals becoming champions of a cause that could become detrimental to the project. As individual members of the body, they are politicians and so concerned with getting reelected. Thus, allowing a governmental concern to become an individual politician's concern may put the project manager, the parent organization, and the client in the position of promoting, or undercutting, the political ambitions of that individual—a most unfortunate position. Note that we are focusing on the political body as opposed to departments within government that are considered to be regulatory agencies, as discussed earlier.

THE PROJECT MANAGEMENT KNOWLEDGE AREAS

The management of projects is best thought of as a collection of processes that, when applied in an organized and consistent manner, provides the greatest assurance that the objectives of the project will be met in the most efficient and effective manner. For ease of discussion and application, these processes are organized into nine knowledge areas by which projects are managed: 1) integration, 2) scope, 3) time, 4) cost, 5) quality, 6) human resources, 7) communications, 8) risk, and 9) procurement.

It must be understood that on real projects these processes are not applied linearly or singularly. There are many loops back through these processes as the *progressive elaboration* of the project proceeds, and the precise sequence in which they are applied often varies, depending upon the project and its progress.

These nine knowledge areas are discussed briefly in the following sections with emphasis on the outputs from each process. The reader is referred to the *PMBOK® Guide* for a more complete discussion of the inputs and tools and techniques for each. This book focuses on those aspects of the knowledge areas that are most relevant to the beginning project manager with emphasis on the tools available for managing scope, time, and cost. (*PM 102* also will focus on these aspects.)

Project Integration Management

THOU ART RESPONSIBLE FOR INTEGRATING THE PARTS INTO THE WHOLE.

It takes many elements of human work, materials, equipment, and other resources to produce the product of the project. The project manager is responsible for ensuring that all of these elements work together, first in performing the project and then in the product of the project. Someone will be depending on the results of the effort. This is no more vividly stated than in the lament of the astronaut who said something like, "My life is dependent upon this space ship that is assembled of thousands of parts, each of which was produced by the lowest bidder."

There are three processes in project integration management: plan development, plan execution, and overall change control.

Project plan development is "taking the results of other planning processes and putting them into a consistent and coherent document" (*PMBOK® Guide*). While some of the other processes and their tools and techniques inherently orient the project in the same direction, the project plan is the document that brings all these other efforts into focus. It also provides an opportunity for the project manager to review the outputs of the other processes to ensure that they are consistent, sufficient, and necessary.

The outputs from the other planning processes must be consistent to prevent surprises and unnecessary rework, should the results of varied work efforts fail to interact properly with one another. An example of such an unfortunate event is two modules of a computer hardware, one which assumed that the beginning of the numerical sequence was *zero* while the other assumed that it was *one*. Another is the Mars mission, in which one module measured distances in yards and another in meters.

The outputs must be *sufficient* to provide adequate direction to the project team and ensure that the product of the project will meet all of the client's requirements. For example, planning outputs must include sufficient checks to ensure the quality of the product. Work omitted in the planning stage not only results in demands on contingency funds and schedule time but, in the process, can lead to conflicts later in the project that add to the burdens of the project manager.

The outputs also must be *necessary*, lest the resources committed to the project be used to further agendas not relevant to the project. Too often, functional managers may attempt using a project to obtain equipment, send people for training, and even hire new people—if they can get by with it. The project manager must recognize such attempts and require justification of each questionable item, or at least use it as a bargaining tool to elicit the cooperation of the functional manager on this project.

Plan execution is the major work of the project. It is primarily concerned with all of the work being performed as planned. It must also recognize the need for changes and ensure that they are made in a

Section/Title

Part I: Objectives and Methods
1. Introduction
2. Project Priorities
3. Management Plan
4. Risk Assessment
5. Acquisition Strategy

Part II: Configuration and Performance Parameters
6. Work Breakdown Structure
7. Cost Estimates
8. Schedule

Appendices
A. Project Management Team Member Responsibilities
B. Construction Management Team Member Responsibilities
C. Approvals

Source: *The Preferred Processes—Project Planning and Management*, Sandia National Laboratories (September), p. 41.

FIGURE III.1

Contents of a Project Plan

prudent manner, that the scope of work is adjusted appropriately, and ensure compensation for additional work performed, if appropriate.

Overall change control "is concerned with (a) influencing the factors that create changes to ensure that changes are beneficial, (b) determining that a change has occurred, and (c) managing the actual changes when and as they occur" (*PMBOK® Guide*). It involves updating the project plans, taking corrective action, and documenting lessons learned. Corrective action is key; it is "anything done to bring expected future project performance into line with the project plan." It is one of the major *value added* services of the project manager.

Scope Management

THOU SHALT KNOWEST
WHAT THOU WAS ASKED TO CREATE.

"The scope of a project is the sum of the products and services to be provided as a project" (*PMBOK® Guide*). There are two distinct aspects of scope: product scope and project scope. The first refers to the features and functions to be included in the product of the project, which are expressed in the specifications of the product of the project. The second refers to the work that must be done to deliver that product. We are primarily concerned at this point with project scope. Scope management includes the following processes: initiation, planning, definition, verification, and change control.

The products of the *scope initiation* process include a project charter, identification of constraints and assumptions on both the project and the product of the project, and the assignment of the project manager. Using the capabilities of project management software, the organization should more carefully consider the impact of resource requirements of the project on the potential to implement other projects. Financial resources have always limited the number of projects that can be undertaken by a given organization. The commitment of other resources to one project may be a more serious constraint than mere money. A key scientist, engineer, or even project manager can be the primary constraint. Thus, in corporate strategic planning, the criteria for selecting projects are broadened.

The outputs of *scope planning* include a scope statement, supporting detail, and a scope management plan. The latter may be the most important step in the project as, without adequate management, scope can grow like cancer. One might describe this as Parkinson's Law for Projects: *Scope expands to consume the resources available—and more.* One manager of project managers commented that managing the scope of projects was his most important and troublesome assignment. On the one hand, he had to ensure that the client's needs had been met but also, on the other hand, ensure that any work content not in the originally contracted scope statement, but done, could be billed to the client.

Perhaps the most important output of all the scope management processes is the work breakdown structure (WBS). (It is so important that it is discussed in detail in Chapter VIII.) It is the output of the *scope definition* process.

Scope verification is the process of formalizing acceptance of the project at the completion of the project or any of its phases. Paying attention to it early in the project increases the probability of client satisfaction as well as that of other stakeholders. It is also an excellent check on the previous scope processes. The ultimate objective of any project is its termination; the surest way to successfully terminate a project is to deliver the expected product(s). The time to ensure that this outcome will be achieved is before the budget is exhausted.

Scope change control is vital on fixed price (or cost) projects in business. After all, the objective of being in business is to have a positive difference remaining when costs are subtracted from the revenue received for performing the project. It is inherent in the client's motives to attempt to get as much as possible from the project without incurring additional costs. Thus, the game—and the challenge—is well defined. The better the tools available to manage change, the more effectively this game can be played, and the more likely that good relations will prevail between the project and the client.

Time Management

TARRY NOT, FOR THY CLIENT WAITEST.

The management of time is crucial to the successful completion of a project. In some large projects that run for several years at costs in excess of a billion dollars, finance charges can approach $1 million per day. Even in many smaller projects, especially in a competitive market, it is essential to complete projects on time, or you will lose the edge in the marketplace. Nowhere is this so poignant as in the pharmaceutical industry where a one-week lead in going to market can determine the dominant market share for the life of the drug.

The function of time management has been divided into five processes: 1) activity definition, 2) activity sequencing, 3) activity duration estimating, 4) schedule development, and 5) schedule control. They are discussed briefly here.

Activity definition determines the work content of the project. Each activity requires time, resources, and direction. The product of each activity must be defined to ensure that it meets the requirements of the succeeding activities. To ensure this, it is important that those who have to use the product of an activity have an opportunity to approve the planned as well as the actual product of the activity. This is in conformance with the philosophy of modern quality management that the customer is the next person in the process.

Activity sequencing may be done concurrently with activity definition but should be recognized as a separate process. In general, the sequence should be based only on technological constraints consistent with the objectives of the project. There are often strong motivations to include "ought to," "would like to," or "it would be nice to" types of constraints. However, in general, they should be avoided. If they are included, they should be carefully documented to ensure their recognition—in the event that they lead to unexpected and detrimental consequences to the schedule.

Activity duration estimating "involves assessing the number of work periods likely to be needed to complete each defined activity" (*PMBOK® Guide*). It should be done without consideration of possible time limits on the project as a whole to minimize bias in estimating. It can, and perhaps should, be combined with estimating resources required to perform the activity.

Schedule development begins with critical path calculations that indicate the shortest time in which the project can be performed *based on the current plan*. Often the first calculations will indicate that it will take two to three times as long to perform the project as is available. It will identify the activities that will need to be modified to reduce project duration while also identifying logical relationships that might be changed to shorten total project duration. Often, major reductions in project time can be achieved with only a few changes to the logic and changes in the methods of performing a relatively few activities. The costs of such modifications to the plan will be far less than the all-too-popular strategy: "Put everyone on overtime."

The first calculations will typically ignore the resource requirements. It will be assumed that whatever resources are required will be available at the times required. It will also ignore any desires to use the resources efficiently, such as holding off on bringing an expensive piece of equipment or crew onto the job until there is sufficient work available to make good use of them. These considerations are held in abeyance until a feasible plan is developed, based on activity durations and logical relationships alone.

Schedule control is vital to project success. It is similar to the famous proposition about the relationship between "for want of a nail" and losing the race. A slight delay in one activity can result in lengthening delays throughout the project. Imagine what might happen if, due to a delay in one activity, the following activity must be delayed because a key resource has been scheduled for a major trip and cannot perform the activity until after her return. This scenario could be continued ad nauseam, and occasionally it will happen on a real project.

Cost Management

USE THY TALENTS WISELY
AND THY REWARDS SHALL BE GREAT.

Cost management "includes the processes required to ensure that the project is completed within the approved budget" (*PMBOK® Guide*). It includes the following major functions: resource planning, cost estimating, cost budgeting, and cost control.

Resource planning involves determining what and how many units of what resources (people, equipment, materials, and supplies) should be used to perform each activity, and the total quantities of each resource during each time period over the duration of the project. Inherent is the determination of the technology, methods, and processes that will be used to perform each activity. Major savings are available by having the right resources assigned to the right activities at the right times throughout the project. Methods of determining resource requirements in the past have led to some expensive mistakes. On a project to prepare for manufacturing a new car line, one plant had requisitioned approximately twice as many new hires of one skilled trade and less than half of the number needed of another skilled trade. The resource analysis from a critical path method-type program gave them more accurate requirements.

Cost estimating "involves developing an approximation (estimate) of the costs of the resources needed to complete project activities" (*PMBOK® Guide*). Note the emphasis on uncertainty in this statement. Many managers are accustomed to working in a mass production environment, where industrial engineering techniques can determine with considerable precision the work content of a particular job. Project work often cannot be estimated with nearly the same precision. There are often uncertainties about unexpected circumstances that may be encountered in performing an activity. The activity is not likely to be performed repetitively, so setting a standard from similar observations is impractical. The specific resources that will be available when the activity can be performed are not known with certainty, and the range of capabilities of alternate resources tends to be quite varied. It cannot be expected that cost estimates can even approach the accuracy achieved in mass production. Nevertheless, an estimate is required if control is going to be exercised. The estimate should always be as accurate as possible, consistent with the needs of the project and constraints that may be applicable.

Cost budgeting "involves allocating the overall cost estimates to individual work items in order to establish a cost baseline for measuring project performance" (*PMBOK® Guide*). The cost-flow pattern for projects is different than for mass production. Rather than being approximately linear over time, in a project, the amount of work and hence the costs vary substantially over time. Typically, the number of resources that can be applied to a project starts low, builds to a peak, and then reduces to zero when the project is completed. This results in a cumulative cost curve that is shaped somewhat like the letter "S" and is therefore called the "S" curve.

One of the major benefits of MPM is the increased precision with which costs can be managed over the life of the project. Previously, costs were accumulated with little or no ability to correlate actual costs to date with the value of work actually performed. Thus, it was often several weeks after project completion that a determination could be made as to whether the project was over or under budget. Today, this can be determined with considerable accuracy at any time during the project.

Cost control "is concerned with (a) influencing the factors that create changes to the cost baseline to ensure that changes are beneficial, (b) determining that the cost baseline has changed, and (c) managing the actual changes when and as they occur" (*PMBOK® Guide*). It is a rare project that is performed exactly as planned. Learning is inevitable as the project progresses, both for things directly associated with as well as external to the project. Underground conditions may be different than expected. A strike in the steel industry might make it advisable to change the design to a concrete structure, as was done on the Pontiac Silverdome. A new technology may be introduced that would make the product of the project obsolete even before it is finished. Thus, change is inevitable. The ability to accept changes in the project and manage them effectively is another benefit of MPM.

Quality Management

THY WORKS SHALT CONFORM TO REQUIREMENTS.

The operational definition of quality is simply "conformance to requirements/specifications" (*PMBOK® Guide*). If the requirements for the product of the project are consistent with the client/customer's real or perceived needs, the client/customer is likely to be satisfied with the product of the project. The product either conforms to these requirements or it does not. Quality should not be confused with excellence, luxury, prestige, *gold-plating*, or other terms that describe the product of the project in qualifying degrees. There can be waste involved in producing a product or service that exceeds requirements just as surely as when producing a product that falls short of requirements. This definition of quality is the essential concept on which quality management operates.

It should be noted that this concept of quality should not lead to a static concept of the client/customer's requirements. Just as change is recognized in the management of scope and cost, we must recognize that the client/customer's needs may change over time. It is the project manager's responsibility to manage these changes so that the product delivered by the project conforms to the needs of the client at the time of delivery. This adds assurance that the client/customer will consider the project a success and will call on the project manager's organization to perform other projects.

The concept of a project as a *process* is essential for the application of *process control*—and, more specifically, *statistical* process control— to the management of projects. The concept of the progressive elaboration of specifications as the essential nature of this process fits with the quality concept that "the customer is the next person/operation in the process" (*PMBOK® Guide*). The "customer" is the next engineer, tool builder, ad layout person, and so on. If the product going to the customer has no defects, she can perform her tasks in the most efficient manner—and do the right thing right the first time.

It should be noted that this same concept of *conformance* can apply to the project itself as a measure of how well it was planned and executed, relative to the original plan and such things as environmental and safety expectations of society.

Quality management on projects consists of planning, assurance, and control.

Quality planning "involves identifying which quality standards are relevant to the project and determining how to satisfy them" (*PMBOK® Guide*). These standards may be the client's but may also include those of the trade and governments.

Quality assurance "is all the planned and systematic activities implemented within the quality system to provide confidence that the project will satisfy the relevant quality standards" (*PMBOK® Guide*). It should include evaluation of the project plan itself, the processes used in performing activities, and skills of personnel performing the work.

Quality control "involves monitoring specific project [and process] results to determine if they comply with relevant quality standards and identifying ways to eliminate causes of unsatisfactory results" (*PMBOK® Guide*). We have added process to the definition from the *PMBOK® Guide* to emphasize the proactive approach to quality, ensuring that the processes used are likely to produce the desired outputs. This minimizes inspection costs, costs of errors, and rework costs.

Human Resources Management

YE SHALL LEAD THEM OUT OF CHAOS.

The project manager is responsible for developing a project team, building it into a cohesive group to complete the project. "Human resources management includes the processes required to make the most effective use of the people involved with the project" (*PMBOK® Guide*). It consists of organizational planning, staff acquisition, and team development.

Organization planning "involves identifying, documenting, and assigning project roles, responsibilities, and reporting relationships" (*PMBOK® Guide*). The project manager should correlate this and staff acquisition—especially with regard to core team members—with the development of the project strategy as expressed in the WBS to ensure that the people actually obtained are capable of implementing the strategy effectively. The ideal WBS may imply a person with certain capabilities. The person actually assigned may be better prepared to work within a different WBS strategy.

Staff acquisition "involves getting the human resources needed (individuals or groups) assigned to and working on the project" (*PMBOK® Guide*). There will likely be tradeoffs and much negotiation in this process. The ideal individual for a key position may not be available at the time required or for the length of time required. This could affect not only project strategy but also the time required to perform certain activities. Do not be caught trying to perform the project in the ideal manner with less than the ideal team. In the end, you will be performing the project with less than the ideal team, so be sure to make adjustments in your project plan and perhaps renegotiate your commitments as to schedule and deliverables.

Communication Management

THOU SHALT NOT KEEP THY PEOPLE IN THE DARK.

"Project communications management includes the processes required to ensure timely and appropriate generation, collection, dissemination, storage, and ultimate disposition of project information" (*PMBOK® Guide*). The processes include communications planning, information distribution, performance reporting, and administrative closure.

Communications planning "involves determining the information and communications needs of the stakeholders: who needs what information, when they will need it, and how it will be given to them" (*PMBOK® Guide*). This is a major difference between managing projects and managing most ongoing operations. Generally, information requirements and systems evolve over time. On a project, plans must be established at the outset that will, it is hoped, meet the needs of the project throughout its life. It is often extremely tedious to modify these plans in midstream.

Information distribution "involves making the needed information available to project stakeholders in a timely manner" (*PMBOK® Guide*). One solution is to provide all information to all team members. This would be very costly and could prove disastrous if so much time is spent reading new information that the productivity of the team goes to zero. On the other hand, lack of critical information could lead to work proceeding based on inappropriate guidance. Many organizations are struggling with balancing information availability with need to know using the new technologies available in information systems and telecommunications today.

Performance reporting "involves collecting and disseminating performance information to provide stakeholders with information about how resources are being used to achieve project objectives" (*PMBOK® Guide*). It includes status and progress reporting and forecasting future status and progress. Many of the tools of MPM are specifically designed to facilitate gathering this information with greater precision than previously available.

Administrative closure "consists of verifying and documenting project [or phase] results to formalize acceptance of the product of the project by the sponsor, client, or customer. It includes collection of project records, ensuring that they reflect final specifications, analysis of project success and effectiveness, and archiving such information for future use" (*PMBOK® Guide*).

Successful project managers are constantly building consensus or confidence in decisions at critical junctures in a project by practicing active communication skills. The project manager must be a communicator to upper management, the project team, and other stakeholders. The communication process is not always easy because the project manager may find barriers to communication, such as a lack of clear communication channels outside the immediate project team and problems with the technical language that must be used. The project manager is responsible for knowing what kind of messages to send and to whom to send them, as well as for translating the messages into a language that can be understood.

Risk Management

BE YE NOT FOOLHARDY;
NEITHER SHALL YE SHRINK FROM OPPORTUNITY.

"Risk management includes the processes concerned with identifying, analyzing, and responding to project risk. It includes maximizing the results of positive events and minimizing the consequences of adverse events" (*PMBOK® Guide*). It is the formal process whereby risk factors are systematically identified, assessed, and provided for. The term *risk management* itself tends to be misleading because management implies control of events. On the contrary, risk management must be seen as preparation for possible events in advance, rather than simply reacting to them as they happen. With time in hand, it is possible to identify alternative action plans and select one that is most consistent with project objectives. Risk management is composed of the following processes: identification, quantification, response development, and response control.

Risk identification "consists of determining which risks are likely to affect the project and documenting the characteristics of each" (*PMBOK® Guide*). Risk may be associated with the project or the product of the project. On one construction project, weather was identified as a risk; the site was impossible to drain adequately and became quite muddy when it rained. The response was to pave the area and perform the construction from that base, which prevented substantial project delays. On the Northumberland Bridge, ice flows were identified as a major source of risk to the bridge piers. A special design for these piers was tested extensively to ensure their ability to withstand this threat. An overly simplified view of risk is to consider only the uncertainties reflected in activity and project durations. Lateness in completing a contract with a penalty clause is certainly a risk. However, risk identification should be more comprehensive.

Risk quantification "involves evaluating the risks and risk interactions to assess the range of possible outcomes" (*PMBOK® Guide*). One of the results of paying more attention to risk management is greater reliance on the tools of decision theory. Thus, the project manager must be much more aware of this area of management knowledge.

Risk response development "involves enhancement steps for opportunities and responses to threats" (*PMBOK® Guide*). It includes avoidance, mitigation, and acceptance. Avoidance might consist of using a proven instead of a state-of-the-art component. Risk mitigation might consist of starting development on two or more alternatives, selecting the most suitable one after at least one is proven to be satisfactory. Acceptance might involve proceeding with construction in a flood-prone area, taking some measures to reduce the loss if a flood does occur.

Risk response control is exercised when a risk event occurs. Efforts are exercised to energize the planned actions to deal with the event, revise the actions in view of the actual occurrence, and update the risk management plan based on lessons learned.

Procurement Management

SEEK YE THE COMPETENT, DEPENDABLE, AND HONEST SUPPLIER.

Inherent in the process of managing a project is the procurement of a wide variety of resources. In most instances, this requires the negotiation of a formal, written document, generally called a contract. Even projects undertaken entirely within a single organization should use a form of contract ensuring cooperation of all stakeholders and minimizing adverse consequences of any delays or failures. Thus, procurement management is essential knowledge. It is composed of six processes: 1) procurement planning, 2) solicitation planning, 3) solicitation, 4) source selection, 5) contract administration, and 6) contract closeout.

Procurement planning "is the process of identifying which project needs can be best met by procuring products and services outside the project organization" (*PMBOK® Guide*). Central to this are make-or-buy decisions and contract type selections.

Solicitation planning "involves preparing the documents needed to support solicitation" (*PMBOK® Guide*). It requires expert knowledge of legal and quasi-legal requirements as applicable in the jurisdiction within which the project is to be performed. It may include multiple jurisdictions on many projects. The entire procurement process can be expedited by qualifying providers before opening the bidding process. In the extreme, one builder used a *family of subcontractors* with whom there was a mutual dependency. Thus, the bidding process was expedited.

Solicitation "involves obtaining information (bids and proposals) from prospective sellers on how project needs can be met" (*PMBOK® Guide*).

Source selection "involves the receipt of bids or proposals and the application of the evaluation criteria to select a provider" (*PMBOK® Guide*).

Contract administration "is the process of ensuring that the seller's performance meets contractual requirements" (*PMBOK® Guide*). Different types of contracts are likely to elicit different types of behaviors from both the contractor and the contractee. They need to be matched to the requirements of the project. The processes of initiating, evaluating, negotiating, and administering contracts are essential skills. In a global business environment, it is also essential to understand varying social, political, legal, and financial implications in this process.

SUMMARY

Based on the foregoing, managing a project may seem overwhelming. It can be if attempted by a person not knowledgeable and skilled in the concepts and techniques identified in the *PMBOK® Guide*. It can also be overwhelming to a person who lacks some essential characteristics for performing as a project manager. The latter will be discussed in the next three chapters.

There are means available for interested persons to learn concepts and techniques; skills must be developed by experience and special types of training. Fortunately, the knowledge and skills of trainers and teachers of project management are improving. It is the OC's opinion that only those trainers and consultants who are certified project management professionals (see Preface) should be called upon for this assistance.

It is also important for managers and executives to understand that MPM is very demanding today, so those selected to manage projects must have training and progressive learning experiences under the guidance of persons with proven abilities in managing projects utilizing MPM.

PMI can provide much guidance and assistance to both individuals and organizations in understanding the requirements of effective MPM and their implementation of this increasingly important approach to managing the enterprise.

Sam was so excited about this newfound knowledge that he wanted to share it with everyone who might work on projects in the future. He found the largest tree in the compound and attached the tablet to it.

COMMANDMENTS OF MPM

I. THOU ART RESPONSIBLE FOR INTEGRATING THE PARTS INTO THE WHOLE.

II. THOU SHALT KNOWEST WHAT THOU WAS ASKED TO CREATE.

III. TARRY NOT, FOR THY CLIENT WAITEST.

IV. USE THY TALENTS WISELY, AND THY REWARDS SHALL BE GREAT.

V. THY WORKS SHALT CONFORM TO REQUIREMENTS.

VI. YE SHALT LEAD THEM OUT OF CHAOS.

VII. THOU SHALT NOT KEEP THY PEOPLE IN THE DARK.

VIII. BE YE NOT FOOLHARDY; NEITHER SHALL YE SHRINK FROM OPPORTUNITY.

IX. SEEK YE THE COMPETENT, DEPENDABLE, AND HONEST SUPPLIER.

APPENDIX III.A—
MARS PATHFINDER PROJECT

The Mars Pathfinder Project received worldwide publicity for its technical and project management achievements. PMI recognized it as the project of the year for 1998. Excerpts from the Jet Propulsion Laboratory's submission for this award are included in this book to illustrate excellence in the application of MPM. This is the first of those edited excerpts.

Summary of Project

On 4 July 1997, the Mars Pathfinder spacecraft landed on the surface of Mars, marking the first visit by a spacecraft to the surface of the red planet since the Viking missions in 1976. The following day, the Sojourner Rover rolled down its deployment ramp and became the first autonomous vehicle to traverse the surface of another planet. During its nearly three months of operation on the surface of Mars, Sagan Memorial Station and Sojourner transmitted 2.6 gigabits of science and engineering data. This included over 16,000 lander camera images; 550 rover camera images; 8.5 million individual temperature, pressure, and wind measurements; 16 separate chemical measurements of Martian rocks and soil; and the results of 10 technological experiments on the rover. The science data collected from the surface and atmosphere has added significant new information to man's understanding of Mars. In addition to the technical achievement, the Mars Pathfinder Mission has been a worldwide public outreach success, recording over 735 million hits on our Pathfinder websites.

Mars Pathfinder received its formal development go-ahead in November 1993 from NASA's Office of Space Science. The mission was conceived as an engineering demonstration of a reliable, low-cost system for delivering payloads to the surface of Mars with highly focused science objectives.

The Pathfinder flight system was designed as a three-in-one spacecraft with a passive entry, descent, landing (EDL) system to enter and descend directly through the Martian atmosphere. ... The three-in-one spacecraft design consisted of a cruise stage, an entry vehicle (with a blackshell and aeroshell), and a tetrahedral shaped lander. ...

The lander carried a suite of instruments (color stereo imaging camera, ASI Met weather station, and dust magnets) and a free-ranging robotic rover to perform science investigations and technology experiments. ...

Mars Pathfinder was part of the NASA Discovery Program, an initiative for "better, faster, cheaper" missions with a maximum three-year development cycle and a cost cap of $150 million in FY '92 dollars ($171M real year). The Sojourner Rover was funded separately by NASA's Advanced Concepts and Technology Office at a cost cap of $25 million. The mission's operations phase was funded separately at $13.9 million.

The challenge presented by these cost and schedule requirements is put in perspective when one considers that the two Viking missions, which landed on Mars in 1976, had a six-year development period and a combined development cost of $915 million (equivalent of $3 billion in FY '92 dollars). Due to its low cost and short development schedule, Pathfinder required a unique spacecraft design and a creative project plan to achieve mission success. ...

The Mars Pathfinder Project distinguished itself in many ways by applying innovative project management techniques. Mission success was accomplished by focusing on a limited set of objectives, streamlining project approaches and minimizing bureaucratic interference. The following project management practices were key to the success of Mars Pathfinder:

1. Co-locate to Maximize Communication—Effective communication is critical to any project. Pathfinder management co-located approximately one hundred engineers on a single floor of an open landscape building. Co-location ... provided the capability to get together and work problems quickly, without the delay of scheduling formal meetings. It also created a strong bond between coworkers and produced a *family* atmosphere. In fact, the flight system management team was on a first-name basis with nearly every employee, including cognizant engineers, designers, and technicians.

2. Practice Hands-on Management—Management's microknowledge of the technical design, programmatic resources, and margins allowed for rapid decision-making, which was critical for maintaining cost and schedule. Microknowledge, without micromanaging, was essential to the success of Pathfinder in the faster, better, cheaper environment.

3. Take Risks and Succeed by Doing Things Differently—The secret to success in the Pathfinder environment of faster, better, cheaper constraints was to be intelligent about taking risks by doing things differently. Part of the reasons for Pathfinder's success was its early designation as a Class C project. This meant that the project had a smaller subset of Jet Propulsion Laboratory (JPL) policies and procedures to follow, and more leeway to concentrate on the most critical aspects of the mission. Making the people, not the policy, responsible for the system being reliable was critical to success.

4. Develop and Maintain an Atmosphere of Openness and Honesty—An atmosphere of openness, honesty, and personal responsibility by every member of the Pathfinder team was essential to our success throughout all phases of development and operations. Project management set the tone for how people worked together by encouraging all team members, regardless of level, to speak their mind and surface problems they uncovered along the way. This spirit of cooperation also carried over into the budget arena, where systems managers would offer budget underruns in their areas to help another system manager who was faced with a budget problem.

5. Use Peer Reviews—Mars Pathfinder held more than one hundred peer reviews covering all elements of the project. Preparations for these reviews forced the project team to be more thorough, anticipate problems, and do the work needed to answer the tough questions that peers will ask. In addition, the use of senior, highly experienced hardware engineers to perform walkthroughs during key stages of final assembly was invaluable in finding and fixing problems.

6. Soft Projectization—Team members from the JPL technical divisions remained administratively tied to their home division, but were directly accountable to the project for performance, cost, and schedule.

7. Emphasize the Hiring and Development of Generalists—Pathfinder management hired a team of engineers who were cross-disciplinary. This allowed the total staff to be much smaller than for similar projects in the past. It also allowed for faster decision-making and less inefficiency during the transition between different phases of the project. Transitioning designers/builders into the testers/operators saved time and reduced risk. Having a team of generalists also made it easier to cross-train workers.

8. Get the Most Out of Team Meetings—Pathfinder meetings did not defer solutions to problems during meetings; many were solved in real time. Having a reputation for making decisions in real time at meetings also encouraged team attendance.

9. Centralized Data Management—The Pathfinder project implemented a centralized data management system to be able to share information between team members more efficiently. ...

Chapter IV

The Project Manager—
Technical Skills*

"Oh my, what have I gotten myself into now?" asked Sam. "I've never built a raft before. I have no experience in building such a large vehicle. All I've ever done is hunt, fish, pick berries, cook, and shape rocks. What do I do now?"

Sam recalled that an earlier encounter had revealed the theory that "you become a project manager one zero at a time." If that is true, there must be certain things that need to be learned first. What could they be? One guru provided a Skills Inventory that included technical, leadership, and administrative skills of the project manager. Sam's first concern was with the technical part of the job. The first stop was the Temple of Technical Expertise on the ivy-covered mountain.

Projects are ubiquitous. Projects must be managed. Ergo, project managers are ubiquitous.

Indeed, it is the rare individual who has not managed a project of some sort. Building a house is certainly a project; moving into it is also a project. Designing a new car is a project; rebuilding an old car is

---

*Much more can be said about technical management; however, it is not the primary focus of this book.

also a project. Adding a new member to the family is a project, whether it is a child, parent, or pet. The number and variety of projects undertaken by individuals are endless and occur throughout life. Each is managed to one degree or another.

Thus, we have all been, and all are, project managers to one degree or another.

So why all the fuss?

Consider one type of project with which we are all familiar: moving. When you moved into your own room (a project), the project manager was probably your mother. When you moved away to college (a project), there may have been some question as to who was really the project manager, you or your mother. When you moved into your first apartment (a project), you were the project manager. Then you moved into a house (another project). Who was the project manager on that one? Each of these projects was larger in magnitude, cost, duration, and complexity than the previous one. The skills and knowledge required for effectively and efficiently performing them were progressively greater.

Some people, lacking the time or skills to manage such a project, turn to someone else to manage their move, to take everything off of every shelf and out of every closet, and put it all in its proper place in the new location. The expectations for these professionals are often greater than we have for ourselves. Thus, they must be skilled in determining what is expected of them and in planning, executing, and closing the project. This is an especially challenging task, because we often do not understand the pending project well enough to state our requirements with any precision; therefore, we tend to make changes to those requirements as the project progresses. This may be acceptable on a small project where we are spending relatively small amounts of our own money. However, the larger the project and the more people involved, the more important it is that the project manager be skilled, not only in the technologies involved (packing dishes, for example) but also in managing the processes involved.

This illustrates an interesting hypothesis about how you become a project manager: one zero at a time. Most professionals get an opportunity to manage a project early in their careers. The first one may involve a few thousand dollars. If it is managed successfully, the next one may be in the tens of thousands of dollars, then the next in the hundreds of thousands, and so on. Thus, if you aspire to be a project manager of large projects, the best advice is to be prepared to manage the first one very well—then the next one and the next one. If you are really good, and fortunate, you may move even faster.

Sam was not the first, nor will he be the last, to have that experience. But what is the right stuff? Centuries later, learned scholars asked the same question. One professor summarized the results of six professors into three major skill categories: 1) leadership/interpersonal, 2) technical, and 3) administrative (Thamhain 1991). While they will be used for discussion, another interesting and useful taxonomy has been referenced to enhance this discussion (Petersen 1991).

INTRODUCTION

In the past, the primary requirement for the person *in charge* of a project was technical competency. A typical title was *project engineer*, *lead systems analyst*, or *chief scientist*. Their responsibilities generally were not defined as overall for the project; thus, they tended to emphasize the technical aspects of the project. While they may have had inherent leadership skills, they were seldom trained or educated in this area. They may have demonstrated some administrative skills, but probably had little interest in performing them. Therefore, many aspects of managing the project were either not attended to or were given less than optimum attention. In many instances, the OC has observed projects managed by a committee or by an executive who could not give the project the required attention to tend to the full range of issues required today.

Today's project manager requires a balanced capability in all three areas: 1) technical, 2) leadership, and 3) administrative. The career path for development of project managers can be through demonstrated competency in any of these. Nevertheless, demonstrated technical competence is most often the primary path.

This first project may involve a total expenditure of $1,000 or so. While you will be performing in all three of these areas, technical competency will be essential at this level. Do it as well as you can! Remember that you are producing two things in the process: the product of the project, and your boss' faith in you. If you perform well, you may be trusted with a $10,000 project, which requires applying a broader repertoire of technologies. You will have more to learn and demonstrate. Success at this level will likely lead to a $100,000 project. The broadening range of technologies involved will require a different type of knowledge. However, your reputation, for the greater part of your career, will depend on the technical expertise you demonstrated in these early projects.

Note that the better you perform across all three skill areas—leadership, technical, and administrative—the more likely you are to move ahead faster than "one zero at a time."

THE SKILL AREAS

Communicating with Technical People

Communicating with technical people requires most of the same skills that are required to communicate with other people. To communicate effectively with technical people, you also need to understand their technical concepts.

Few people can be competent in more than a few technologies, but, with proper formal and informal education, they can understand the key concepts and principles. If your project involves the application of physical sciences, such as in engineering, it is helpful to understand physics and chemistry. The more you understand, the better. If the project involves social sciences, such as marketing or advertising, it is important to understand general psychology and sociology, as well as consumer behavior.

In general, the less you understand of the other person's vocabulary, the more likely you are to be *snowed*, and the less likely you are to gain the respect of that person.

Technical Credibility

Whatever the nature of the project, the project manager must have sufficient knowledge of the technologies involved to comprehend the problems involved. If the project involves engineering, the project manager must be able to demonstrate skills in at least one engineering discipline. If the project is creating a stage production, the project manager must be skilled in at least one aspect of the theater. In the beginning, you will be given a small piece of the project to manage. Indeed, you will probably do it all yourself, coordinating your activities with others who have a stakeholding interest in that small part.

Understanding of Technology and Trends

Projects are the means for creating things for the future. On the largest, longest-duration projects, the product of the project may be obsolete before the project is completed. The project manager is often torn between accepting the current proven technology and taking the risk involved in adopting the technology that is state of the art now and more likely to be a relevant technology when the project is finished. What are the risks? State-of-the-art technologies may increase the duration and cost of the project and may in fact fail. On the other side of the coin, older, proven technologies may fail to meet the performance requirements of increasingly demanding projects. You must plan your reading and attendance at technical meetings carefully to ensure that you broaden your understanding of the range of technologies and their trends.

Understanding the Tools and Methodologies of Relevant Technologies

Each technology has its own repertoire of tools and methodologies. You need not be able to use each of them, but you must be able to understand their nature and underlying principles.

For example, if the project involves metallurgy, you need not be able to run a hardness test, but it would be well to know that a *Brinell* is a measure of metal hardness. If the project is a stage production, you need not be able to properly light a set, but you do need to recognize that a *klieg* is a high-intensity light. This level of understanding will help you understand what is involved in meeting an objective. It will also enhance the image that others on your team have of you, and it will further reduce the probability of them being able to snow you.

Ability to Manage the Technology

Understanding a technology is not the same as being able to manage that technology. Consider the *simple* technology of data analysis known as linear regression analysis (LRA). With the simplest knowledge of LRA, you will be able to understand a projection into the future based on the *ceteris paribus* (all other things equal) assumption. If you are going to make a decision based on LRA, it would be advisable to know the five assumptions underlying the LRA model. It would be even better to know that there are tests to determine if any of these assumptions have been violated. You need not be able to perform those tests, but you should be able to ask questions about their results. For example, one of those assumptions is that the relationship between the independent and dependent variable is linear; i.e., it looks like a straight line. Often, one look at the plotted data can provide a *gut reaction* about this assumption. Performing the appropriate test can give an answer that is far more reliable.

Aid in Problem Solving

Working with your team members to aid in problem solving can be demanding. If it goes beyond aid, it weakens the team's ability to solve problems on its own. Don't jump in too fast! Consistent failure to aid will lead team members to seek the help of others, thus weakening your ability to lead the team. Today, no one person can possess the expertise to solve all problems on a project. One person can learn to be a good listener and ask questions using the standard reportorial words: what, where, when, why, and how. Consider the impact of comments such as:

❑ Tell me what you are trying to do.
❑ Tell me how you are doing it.
❑ What are the results?
❑ Why are the results not correct?
❑ Who can we call to help us understand the problem?

In most cases, the problem will be solved before asking the last question. Occasionally, you will be lucky and, often because you are less deeply involved, be able to identify the key factor causing the problem. Luck has been on the OC's side on many occasions, especially with computer program debugging. Although never a great programmer, ability to read code and see logical inconsistencies enabled him to identify coding problems quickly, sometimes to the consternation of some subordinates.

This ability to comprehend what others are doing may well be the key to aiding in problem solving.

Facilitating Tradeoffs

Earlier, we stated that the essence of project management is the integration of the elements of the project, which takes place in both the human and technical dimensions. In the human dimension, these tradeoffs involve reallocating or reassigning resources to ensure that they are adequate for both the work content and technical skill requirements. In the technical dimension, they involve reallocating technical performance requirements for components to ensure that the overall technical performance requirements of the product of the project are met in the most economical manner. This may require assessment of alternative technologies, methodologies, suppliers, materials, or components. The more complex the project, the less likely you are going to be able to perform such tradeoffs. You will have to rely on other members of the team to bring their technical expertise to bear. You may even have to go outside the team and even the organization. What you will have to bring to bear in this analysis is the specification of the problem, the format in which information is to be presented, and the systems perspective. The latter is discussed below.

Two errors that can be made in specifying the problem are focusing on symptoms and focusing on a single technology or component. Too often in both management and technical situations, the obviousness of symptoms can lead to myopia and failure to see the true problem. You must insist that the team stop long enough to assess this matter. Focusing on a single technology or component is tempting for two reasons. Team members will tend to perceive the situation from the perspective of their dominant disciplines. Thus, an electrical engineer will bring to bear the most familiar tools and methodologies. On the other hand, some people will be glad to accept that it is an electrical engineering problem, so they do not have to accept any responsibility for finding the solution.

System Perspective

The larger and more complex the project, the more important it is to have a systems perspective. Interestingly, this perspective is not held by a majority of people. Many years ago, an academic friend researched this question for a population of engineers. He developed a questionnaire that was able to distinguish the systems thinkers from the nonsystems thinkers. Only about 10 percent of the subjects had this capability. Very simply, the systems thinker is able to conceive of the final product of the project as an integrated whole.

Dr. Jay Forrester, then at Massachusetts Institute of Technology, once said something like, "The only really valuable education for management is electrical engineering." Forrester was reflecting on the notion that electrical engineering is taught in the dynamic mode of a flow process, which is a relevant observation for the systems way of thinking. The systems thinker is able to consider the dynamic nature of things.

Understanding of Market and Product Applications

The greater the number of zeros in the total project budget, the greater the need for the project manager to understand the market for and the application of the product. For one thing, there are more variables, including greater investment and longer lead time, until realization of a return on investment. All these contribute to greater risk for the sponsor.

Sensitivity to the concerns of the sponsor and skill in dealing with these concerns can lead to greater satisfaction of the sponsor upon completion of the project.

Integrating Technical, Business, and Human Objectives

It is no longer sufficient to complete the project on schedule, within budget, and achieve the required technical performance. It must also be accomplished in a manner that is consistent with other business objectives. For example, failure to meet guidelines for minority contracting or environmental requirements can cause both the project team and the sponsor considerable headaches—if not more serious troubles. Failure to meet health and safety expectations can cause the job to be shut down—and even business failure of the project contractor. In some jurisdictions, failure to deal adequately with labor agreements can lead to interminable delays and excessive costs.

Unifying the Technical Team

This becomes increasingly demanding as the magnitude of the project increases. The project alignment process was developed to facilitate conveying of the project sponsor's expectations to the project team. But that is not enough. It must be a continuing process, as obstacles met and opportunities revealed during the project will inevitably lead to changes. These changes must be conveyed to the team in a manner that reaches the subconscious, so they become the prevalent way of thinking about the project.

Maintaining momentum on a project is always a challenge. The larger the project, the greater the challenge. Many project managers are using key events in the project as a cause for celebration. The Bad Creek-pumped hydro used this approach very effectively (Snyder and Caligan 1990). Darnall describes an outstanding project in which the project manager promised to swim across a pond on company property—in the middle of February—if certain demanding goals were met (1996). They were, he did, and all had fun. Other techniques have been described in various articles over the years.

Fostering an Innovative Environment

For many project managers, an *innovative project environment* is an oxymoron. Although project management is about the managing of change, change itself can be the greatest source of risk on a project. Often the full implications of the change are not understood, not all affected people are informed, and unintended consequences are discovered. Thus, it is easy to understand the aversion to change initiated through innovation. On the other hand, many projects have been successful precisely because of innovative solutions to major problems. Effective change control and communication are essential for this to happen consistently.

Having resolved the project manager's mindset problem, how do you foster innovation? Perhaps it is easier to talk about how easy it is to destroy such an environment. Chewing out a project team member for making an error while attempting innovation is a sure way. The wound has already been suffered; rubbing salt in it will only make it hurt worse. It is far better to make the error a positive learning experience by taking the time to analyze what happened and how to prevent it the next time.

SUMMARY

Technical skills are essential for the beginning project manager. On small projects, technical tasks likely will be performed by the project manager. If these projects are performed well, responsibility will grow, and, as it does, the relative importance of technical skills is replaced by growing importance of leadership and administrative skills. Demonstrating skills in all three areas will surely enhance the career of the aspiring project manager. However, there will be a temptation to continue to be the expert in one's primary technical area. This should be avoided, if possible, for two reasons. First, it will not foster confidence and growth on the part of those upon whom you are depending in that area. Second, it will likely lead to spending too much time on those technical problems and failing to perform the broader responsibilities as project manager.

Another career path for aspiring project managers is growing in recognition and importance. As more educational programs are offered in project management, more graduates are taking positions on project teams where they learn sufficient technical knowledge to allow them to be effective project managers. This is increasing the confidence of management of many organizations to consider such people for increasing responsibilities, even though they are not educated in the relevant technologies. The logic of this trend is clearer when one considers the increasing breadth of knowledge and skill that is being brought to bear on modern-day projects. Thus, leadership and administrative skills may be more important than technical skills for the larger projects.

> Sam breathed a sigh of relief. It was cold up on the mountain, and the wind was blowing. The lessons of the great technical guru had been extensive. On the other hand, the sigh of relief reflected Sam's confidence that many of the technical skills were already in place. Sam was known for his ability to make technically complex concepts simple and enjoyed the respect of others on technical matters. Sam understood the technologies, tools, and methodologies relevant for this project, having cut trees, hunted, and tanned skins. Sam was often looked to for assistance in solving technical problems and could get others to perform their technical tasks, often in innovative ways.
>
> People liked working for Sam, as they always felt that they grew professionally while pursuing the assigned technical and business objectives. Facilitating tradeoffs and systems perspective were strange concepts that Sam found interesting. They would require further study. Thus, the skills necessary for the immediate project were in place. The raft was indeed a possible dream—technically speaking, that is. Sam started preparing immediately for the trek down this mountain and up the next one to learn more about the leadership skills required.

Chapter V

The Project Manager— A Leader

Good leaders take at least a little more than their share of the blame and a lot less than their share of credit.

Unknown

Here I am, a project manager. Do I have the right stuff? There were many that offered suggestions; yet Sam noted a strange inconsistency among these people's opinions. It was time to seek further knowledge.

Sam had a tedious journey up the mountain to the Temple of Mystics. There the Great Guru of Leadership provided some insights that made Sam believe that the raft was really a "possible dream."

LEADERSHIP AND INTERPERSONAL SKILLS

Leadership and interpersonal skills are those necessary to relate to others, persuade them to participate, give them guidance, and ensure that decisions are made when necessary. To some extent, these skills are based on inherent physical and mental characteristics of the individual or on values and behaviors learned after birth. Regardless, training and knowledge can enhance skills. The leadership and interpersonal skills and characteristics are presented here in a sequence representing the priorities that this old hand considers most important. However, an effective project management professional must have at least minimal skills in each of the areas.

Interest in the Job

The first test, although not necessarily the most important, is interest in the job. If there is no interest, the remaining characteristics may be academic. That is not always so. Sometimes our interests change when more information is available. Have you ever experienced the feeling, "No one ever explained it to me that way"? If interest cannot be generated, enthusiasm will wane with the adversity that is inevitable in managing a project.

Action Oriented

For my money, this is the most important of these skills. Action-oriented people are often referred to as self-starters. They are aggressive and assertive, but not obnoxious and intractable. Neither a milquetoast nor a hardhead can be an effective project manager in the long run. The milquetoast, not being able to make a decision or deal with the slightest obstacle, will lose the faith of the team. The hardhead will end up getting sandbagged, inadvertently or deliberately.

Other characteristics that relate to being action oriented are decisiveness, ascendancy (willingness to take command), and need to achieve and be proactive (willingness to exercise control over others). There is another side to this coin, however, which is not often documented in academic research. Seeking responsibility must be accompanied by accepting responsibility. It seems to this observer that accepting responsibility has become a scarce commodity, at least in the United States (U.S). Many people want responsibility, but few are willing to stick it out through the bad times as well as the good. In the short-term-oriented society that characterizes the U.S., it is all too easy to move on to greener pastures when the going gets tough. The

---

On Larry Bird

Note: While writing this chapter, an article appeared in USA Weekend, a magazine supplement to many Sunday newspapers (McCafferty 1998). It was about Larry Bird, the famous Boston Celtic, now coach of the Indianapolis Pacers. This and other quotes in this chapter are from that article. They exemplify good leadership qualities, according to the Olde Curmudgeon.

"While Bird is considered a 'player's coach,' he's no softy. He ordered that a plane take off in October [1998] leaving two tardy players behind, even though he knew they were nearby on the passenger cart."

"Tardiness: 'If they don't show up on time, I'm not waiting around. My time is as important as their time.'

"Patience and teamwork: 'Everyone has to have the same goal, and it ain't going to come overnight.'

"Honesty: Players 'want to hear the truth. That's what I've always been about. If they screw up, I tell them. A lot of folks just throw a lot of B.S. around, and I don't do that.'"

---

outstanding project manager will see the project through, or provide the client with a well-supported recommendation that it be terminated, but he will not leave the client holding the bag.

Tolerance for Ambiguity and Change

The professor says, "ability to manage in an unstructured environment." More directly, you must be able to deal with ambiguity, and bring order out of chaos. Ambiguity can be in the form of contradictory directions from various stakeholders, conflicting requirements that make the job seem impossible, and even a vague statement of requirements and desires. Somehow, the project manager is expected to read minds, operate a Ouija board, and see clearly in a crystal ball.

How does an ordinary human do all this? Sometimes by asking questions; but watch the body language, because a lot of folks don't like to be asked tough questions—especially if they think the answers might be used against them. These folks subscribe to the eleventh commandment: Thou shalt not commit thyself! Others shoot from the hip and give you answers you really don't need.

Probably the best way to deal with this is to overwhelm these people with staff work; i.e., develop the solution you believe to be the best, and provide answers to all possible questions. The advantage of this approach is that soon you will get a reputation for thorough staff work and knowing the right things to do. You will be asked fewer questions. Be sure you are right, though.

Even better is to develop two or more alternative solutions, and present them in clear comparison for your boss or client to make the decision. Be sure to provide a decision deadline, however, or it may take forever to get the decision. A caveat: such thorough preparation may result in you getting more and larger assignments in the future.

Vision

No, this does not mean that you need eyeglasses. It means having a vision of the product of the project and of the project itself. It means having such a clear idea of what your client desires from the project that you can communicate it in a clear and enthusiastic manner. It means believing in the project and wanting it to be the best project ever done. Lack of enthusiasm will be recognized immediately by the project team and all those around you.

Having a clear vision is essential for providing clear direction. Without it, decisions are likely to be inconsistent and often late, priorities will waver, and team members' confidence in their leader will wane.

Objectives and Priorities

The successful project manager establishes clearly defined objectives and priorities. This should be done with the participation of the relevant project team members and stakeholders. Often the relevant group is larger than you think. Those who believe that they have a legitimate role in making a decision but were excluded become the most recalcitrant in implementing the decision. Also, resist the temptation to modify objectives and priorities with every little shift of the winds of organizational politics.

Objectives are clearest when they address three characteristics: 1) attribute, 2) yardstick, and 3) goal (Ansoff 1974). For example, your objective may be to complete the project (attribute), based on a calendar (yardstick), by 3 July (goal). Alternatively, you could have project duration as the attribute, working days as the yardstick, and 105 (working days) as the goal. Until the objective is stated with such clarity, it will not be effective in guiding the project team's behavior.

A popular format for an objective is:

> To (what is to be accomplished) ...
>
> in such a way that (desired characteristics of results) ...
>
> so that (what is the purpose for doing this?) ...
>
> at a cost not to exceed (limits on expenditures).

To be complete, this should really have a statement about the completion time or date. It could be a simple request for the responsible person to develop a plan and schedule for approval.

Team Development

A group of people is subject to the laws of entropy. Left to their own devices, people will tend to go off in all directions, like Pegasus. This is especially true of project teams, as they are characteristically interdisciplinary with each member having different knowledge, skills, and values; come from different organizational and discipline cultures; and often are at different phases in their personal life cycles. Starting with such a group, the project manager must quickly develop a cohesive team with a sufficient set of common values to enable members to work together with a common vision of the journey on which they are about to embark. Responsibilities must be delegated, and the team must be structured to facilitate effective working relations. To accomplish this, the project manager must exercise considerable interpersonal influence, persuasion, and negotiation skills.

On Larry Bird

Larry Bird's "management style: 'I'm not a screamer. My whole thing is pre-paredness. ... We work these guys in practice. But I feel that once the game starts, let the players play the game. [If] a coach talks too much once the game starts, they don't listen.'"

Motivate People

Having initiated the team development process, the project manager must motivate team members and other participants to apply their best efforts and energies to meet the project objectives. Eliciting commitment and creating personal involvement at all levels by understanding the professional needs of and showing consideration toward individual team members does this.

Many old-timers still believe that the opportunity for continued employment is sufficient motivation to perform. That may be true for those who have no alternative, but few professionals fall in that class. Furthermore, reliance on that crutch will hardly ever motivate a team to that outstanding performance that results in an excellent performance rating for the project manager.

Managing Conflict

Conflict is inherent in projects as a result of the many decisions that must be made and the diversity of project team members. Managed conflict on a project can lead to innovative time- and cost-saving solutions to problems. Unmanaged conflict will probably result in chaos and failure. The project manager must have not only the *stomach* for managing conflict, but also a deep understanding and honed skills in resolving conflict. Perhaps the most difficult skill is ferreting out the existence of conflict, since people are generally reluctant to bring it to the boss' attention. The adroit project manager will ask questions in such a way as to force the issues onto the table.

Assisting in Decision-Making

It is a real temptation for many project managers to become too involved in decision-making. The result will be the opportunity to make even more decisions and become the major bottleneck on the project—always on the critical path. This will lead to neglecting those responsibilities that are uniquely the project manager's. Once this vortex starts to form, unless dramatic action is taken, the project is destined to go down the drain.

The operative word is *assist*. The project manager must allow the appropriate person or group to identify, analyze, and solve the problem, stepping in only to provide information not otherwise available or presenting alternative decision-making theory or techniques. This does not relieve the project manager of final responsibility for the decision; it must be reviewed. Thus, the project manager must ensure that the decision-making process is adequately documented, to permit timely review, and filed for future reference in the event of changes or claims.

Gaining Organizational Support

Ideally, an essential element of project success is the support of upper management, at least of relevant upper management. Sometimes this is instantly available. At other times, your project may be of only passing interest to upper management. Sometimes you will be happy if upper management members are at least neutral to your project. Nevertheless, your future will depend on your success on this project.

Regardless, there are techniques and approaches to elicit support. First among these is to understand the organization and key people in it. It is important to know the formal policies and procedures, but perhaps more important to know the informal ones. At least equally important is to know the key influence leaders in all levels of the organization. On more than one occasion, the essential person has been a custodian or secretary. The astute project manager does not ignore these people in the rush to impress.

On Larry Bird

Larry Bird on motivation: "It was a small gesture, a detail anyone could have forgotten. Indiana Pacers forward Austin Croshere, 22, is an NBA rookie whose clutch play in college prompted comparisons to the great Larry Bird. Which is fine, except that the great Larry Bird is now his coach, and Croshere's play hasn't resembled anything approaching his boss' playing career.

But in January, a shot from the struggling Croshere found its way into an NBA basket for the first time. Coach Bird remembered to give the ball to the rookie before they boarded the team bus. Ask Bird about it now and he shrugs. 'He'll have grandkids one of these days,' Bird says. 'A lot of players go through games and have nothing to show for it other than the record books. Well, he's got the ball.'

No big deal. Except Bird doesn't have *his* ball. No coach thought to grab it when he scored his first pro basket in 1979. 'I wish they did,' he says quietly."

Also, it is important to know the sensitive issues for each key person. The wrong statement or question in her presence can instantly convert a passive stakeholder into an active obstacle. In short, the project manager must learn to engage in organizational politics, not harmfully but constructively. Politics is not a nasty word to be avoided, but rather it is an inherent aspect of organized human behavior.

Communicating

The project manager must be a skilled communicator, both orally and in writing. The greater the magnitude of the project, the more critical it is to the organization, and the larger the number of stakeholders, the greater the skill required. The most important skill is knowing when and what to communicate. Timing is critical. Bad news can be tempered with good news.

Failure to communicate may result in your boss being blindsided, a sure way to *lose friends and influence people* to turn you out to other pastures. Attempt to communicate too much and you will lose your audience. Use visual aids, and keep communication brief. Seek the help of professional communicators if available. Otherwise, seek out a trusted associate to listen to your presentation or proofread your report.

Having Credibility

Honesty, integrity, and loyalty are critical if you are going to be credible. These characteristics may be in conflict in some instances. Exercising tact may be the only option. Protecting your credibility should be of the highest priority. Once your credibility is in question, your support will be eroded. If destroyed, it will be a long, hard battle to regain it. Consider the faith that others place in you to do the things you promise, to be correct in the things you say, and to support those who depend on you. Then put yourself in the other person's position. The answers should be clear.

Visibility

A popular concept in management today is *managing by walking around*. First, you are more likely to know what is really happening. Second, you convey your interest in the project, and that interest is contagious. Third, with some preparation and practice, you can demonstrate your interest in individual needs of team members. Fourth, many team members will communicate more frankly with you in their own environments rather than in your office. Fifth, you are more in control of your time, as you can leave the area when you wish, while it is more difficult to get people out of your office.

General Interpersonal Skills

Many who find themselves in management positions arrive there with no formal training in interpersonal behavior—other than that attained from their parents or on the playground.

"Who needs it?" you ask. "I've been getting along with people all my life!" Yeah! Right! If that is all it takes, then why is your boss such a. ... ?

Getting along with others is not an innate characteristic with which all people are born. It is a skill and an art that is learned, and, just as in

---

On Larry Bird

Larry Bird on responsibility: "His formula, simple and direct, would work well in today's high-octane workplace: Prepare well, play hard and come to work on time. Bird hires good people and lets them do their job."

---

golf, a qualified instructor can improve your swing enough to take several strokes off your game. Have you ever known someone to whom you would recommend, "Enroll in a Dale Carnegie course and just keep repeating it until you can pass it"? Don't be cocky in this area. You too can be helped, and it may improve your score in the project management game.

SUMMARY

Various studies have verified the importance of these characteristics. If you have them, you may aspire to a career, or at least a stint, as a project manager. If you really do not like any of these characteristics, you should probably seek an alternate career. In between, you should set realistic aspiration levels for the magnitude and complexity of projects you would like to manage. Most people can manage some level of project. As in other aspects of life, only those who excel in these characteristics will ultimately progress to the largest, most complex, and most important projects.

Perhaps you feel weak in some areas. Training and/or education can help your development. Experience is always a good teacher, although it is sometimes more painful and slower than a more formal approach. Experience need not be limited to employment opportunities; there are countless community and other organizations that desperately need leaders. You could obtain an opportunity to develop skills and knowledge generally by only mentioning that you might like to help. Valuable experience and training can be obtained through such organizations as Toastmasters International, dedicated to helping individuals learn how to communicate.

These opportunities are available to everyone. Seeking them out and becoming involved should be considered as the first step in proving your *interest in the job* (i.e., being a project manager) and in being action oriented.

> Sam reviewed the lessons of the Great Guru of Leadership and how they were relevant to the immediate project. He was definitely interested in managing this first major raft project and was known to be action oriented. Sam felt challenged by ambiguity and change, having often sought opportunities to be involved in unique undertakings.
>
> Sam enjoyed 20/20 vision! [No, no, that was just a test to see if you were paying attention.] People often came to Sam asking, "How can we do this? What will it look like?" Sam would always break down that vision into smaller manageable tasks and assign priorities, so they would know exactly what to do first, second, and so on. Despite their many opinions, Sam would always leave these people with a feeling of belonging to a team, motivated to get their job done.
>
> Sam enjoyed creating productive conflict to get the best ideas from all of the team members but avoided making all the decisions, opting to let the team learn from that experience. Sam's skill in gaining organizational support and visibility was largely due to skills in communicating and having credibility. It was generally recognized that a task given to Sam would be completed in a timely manner and achieve the desired objectives. Finally, Sam's general interpersonal skills were as good as anyone in the community.
>
> After this review, Sam felt much better. The essential technical and leadership skills were in place. Now it was time to turn attention to the administrative skills.

APPENDIX V.A—
MARS PATHFINDER PROJECT

Mars Pathfinder management realized early that the most important factor in the success of the mission would be putting together a talented team of people who could work together in an environment that would foster innovation and dedication. The team of Jet Propulsion Laboratory, National Aeronautics and Space Administration, and contractor personnel was highly skilled and totally committed to the success of the mission. The challenge associated with new ways of doing business and the willingness of project management to give workers the responsibility and authority to make critical decisions kept employee motivation and morale at a high level throughout the entire project. One of the strengths of the Mars Pathfinder Project was its communication between team members.

The Mars Pathfinder philosophy was to have a flat organization, which would be inherently better for project communications.

The management team was on a first-name basis with nearly every member of the team. Key decisions were able to be made quickly, because the management team communicated constantly with all levels of personnel. It knew the status, problems, problem ramifications, and whether the people were right to fix the problem. A flat organization was found to foster a sense of trust between management and other team members. From the project manager on down, open and honest communication was always encouraged. Everyone on Mars Pathfinder worked for only one goal: mission success. No hidden agendas were tolerated. All team members had access to the state of the budget and reserves. When an account manager could justify the need for reserves, it was granted. There were no arbitrary budget cuts.

Co-location also played a large role in successful communications between the team members. Pathfinder management co-located approximately one hundred engineers on a single floor of an opened landscape building. Co-location of project management, system engineering, attitude, and information management hardware, software and I&T, mission design, and ground data system provided the capability to get together and work problems quickly, without the delay of scheduling formal meetings. It also created a strong bond between coworkers and produced a *family* atmosphere.

Chapter VI

The Project Manager—
Administrative Skills

Sam's journey continued to the next mountain to the Temple of Bureaucracy. There the Great Guru of Scientific Methodology was holding forth on the newfangled tools and techniques for managing projects. Sam soon realized that this stuff was going to be hard to understand. There were new concepts, and a lot of them involved lots of numbers, crazy-looking graphs, and something called probability. But then there were some other things that sounded a bit more familiar. Sam listened intently and found that the further the Great Guru got into the subject, the more interesting it got.

INTRODUCTION

This is the real test of the truly effective project manager. The typical project manager is inclined to be concerned about technical matters of the project, getting things going, and leading the project team to success. The details of administration are often the last to be dealt with. Yet the truly effective project manager must worry about the details of administration. It is necessary to ensure that all of the work defined in the project scope is accomplished, and the product(s) of the project is (are) delivered as promised. It is also necessary to ensure that the budget is spent as planned as well as to schedule the work in a manner that utilizes the right resources at the right time on the right work. It may be very important to provide documentation in the event that there is a dispute requiring proof of prudent decision-making and thorough attention to quality and regulatory requirements.

Following is a discussion of the administrative skills that are important for a project manager to use in the process of executing a project.

THE SKILLS

Communicate Effectively

One of the critical skills that typically differentiates a project manager from a technologist is the ability to communicate both orally and in writing. Many people abhor expressing themselves orally in other than a one-on-one situation. If this is you, forget about becoming a project manager. On the other hand, if you avoid communicating to a group because of a feeling of inadequacy, there are some simple remedies. The first is simply taking advantage of opportunities to speak in low-risk environments. If you want to be more aggressive, you might take one or more courses at a community college. If you really want to be aggressive in developing your speaking capabilities and need a supportive environment, seek a local chapter of Toastmasters International. If writing is difficult, there are some other approaches. Your local community college probably offers a variety of writing courses. Be careful, though; unless your objective is to create fiction, you really need a course in business writing. There is a difference!

Another aid in writing is a personal computer; it is easier to edit and rewrite. The spellchecker can be helpful, but it does not check for meaning, only that the word exists as spelled. For example, both *functional* and *dysfunctional* are legitimate words, but their meanings are quite different. Furthermore, the dictionary contains perfectly legitimate words that could be very embarrassing in public discourse.

The personal computer also helps improve your grammar. The grammar-checking capability can not only improve grammar on a given document but also your knowledge of grammar. To achieve the latter, you must take the time to use the grammar checker carefully; turn on the explanations and read them. If you do not understand them, invest in a reference such as *The Chicago Manual of Style*, which provides a well-indexed guide to the details of grammar.

Another advantage of using a grammar checker is that it will analyze your writing for ease of reading. The Gunning's Fog Index and the Flesch Reading Ease Grade Level are measures of reading difficulty, presented as a number that represents the grade level of your writing. For example, 12 represents the reading level of a person who has successfully completed high school.

Two factors especially contribute to a high reading level: the number of words in a sentence, and the number of words with more than three syllables. Table VI.1 shows how simply splitting one long sentence into two sentences improves these values. In addition, the shorter sentences often make the statement *punchier*—i.e., more likely that the reader or listener will comprehend the point. Even with all of these nice tools, though, you have the ultimate responsibility for what a document says. You must learn the skills of proofreading to be sure that your document says what you intend and that ambiguity is reduced to a minimum. Table VI.2 shows statistics on this chapter.

If you are making an oral presentation, reading-ease concepts become even more critical. A long, complex, convoluted sentence is more likely to be misunderstood when heard than when read. Write your presentation exactly as you plan to give it. Use the grammar checker to aid revising and simplifying.

Present by reading your script, if you wish, but your delivery may seem dry and stilted. A better method is to convert your script into notes and presentation aids. Then you will be able to speak to the group as if you are talking to only one individual. Just be sure to *slow down* and *speak with increased volume*. There is much more to communicating effectively than can be discussed here. Just remember that you are communicating in everything you do: how you dress, behave, look at people, and listen and the tone of your voice. Pay at least as much attention to these means of communicating as to your written and spoken words.

Consider the impact on reading ease if the following sentence is modified:

A. Two factors that contribute to a high reading level are the number of words in a sentence and number of words with more than three syllables.

B. Two factors contribute to a high reading level. They are the number of words in a sentence and number of words with more than three syllables.

Factor	Sentence A	Sentence B
Total words	27	27
Sentences	1	2
Paragraphs	1	1
Syllables	37	37
Three-syllable words	2	2
Words per sentence	27	13.5
Gunning's Fog Index	13.1	8.4
Flesch-Kincaid Score	11.1	5.8
Flesch Reading Ease Score (Maximum = 100)	63.5	77.2
Flesch Reading Ease Grade Level	8.7	7.3

TABLE VI.1

An Example of Improving Reading Ease

Finally, some of the best communications are done with only two words, such as thank you, good job, keep going, and good thinking.

Understand Policies and Procedures

Every organization has policies and procedures to ensure consistency in behavior of all elements of the organization. Most of the time, many of these procedures are designed to help you know what to do in most circumstances. Sometimes they become dated, or they conflict with others that have been changed. Some just should not apply in certain new situations. Nevertheless, intimate knowledge of these documents will reduce the chances of doing something stupid. It is essential that you read all relevant policies and procedures, a chore that will challenge your senses. With a few exceptions, humorous they are not.

Perhaps the most important parts of these documents are the sections that discuss potential deviations from approved policies and procedures. The most important person to know in this case is whoever

Factor	Value
Total words	4,339
Sentences	246
Paragraphs	81
Words per sentence	17.3
Sentences per paragraph	3.8
Passive sentences	11%
Flesch Reading Ease Score (Maximum = 100)	53.4
Flesch Reading Ease Grade Level	9.9

TABLE VI.2
Analysis of Reading Ease of This Chapter

represents your area on committees dealing with important procedures. Knowing the policies and procedures will help you do things right the first time, and knowing the record of deviations and plans for revisions will often enable you to accomplish things that others cannot.

Attract and Hold Capable People

Projects are performed by people; they (except, perhaps, for your first one) are never done by *me*. Never forget that! People will gladly help you if you can be just a little humble, and if you are willing to share the credit. If you are unable to do both, you may notice that one of three things happens. First, people may start avoiding you and your projects. If they cannot accomplish that, they may just stand back, and let you do it by yourself. If you are really *bad*, you may get sandbagged. If that phrase is not familiar to you, maybe you can recall a couple of your *friends* doing it to you. Ever have someone approach you from the front and all of a sudden give you a shove backwards? Only then did you realize that someone else had *sneaked up* and was on hands and knees right behind you. Boom! On a project, it may be done with more finesse, but it will be just as big of a shock and may be far more damaging.

If you subscribe to the management philosophy expressed by some old-timers that "the only motivation people working for me need is the opportunity for continued employment," you may be in trouble. Years ago, this may have worked most of the time, and it may work some of the time today. If it is your approach, though, you may have trouble recruiting really good people. Learn what the people with whom you work really want from their investment in your project. Maybe it is the opportunity to prove their potential in a specific area. You can help them achieve this success and ensure that key people who can make a difference recognize it. On the other hand, maybe they simply want some flextime to allow them time to be a little league baseball coach.

This sort of consideration will not only elicit the cooperation of those on your team, but also the word will get around that you believe in meeting the needs of your people. Soon you will find that the best people want to work on your project. But being considerate by itself will not earn you this respect. People want to work on successful projects, so you must ensure that you develop a reputation for running them.

Successful projects enhance a person's résumé. Good résumés lead to greater opportunities. Helping people strengthen their résumés will gain you all the good help that you need.

Delegate Effectively

If you can divide your projects into assignments that can be effectively delegated, you will minimize your own problems and create opportunities for your project team members. (This responsibility also enhances a résumé.) The key to accomplishing delegation of tasks is the work breakdown structure (WBS), which will be discussed in Chapter VIII.

In the early stages of development, a project manager generally also has responsibility for the technical aspects of assigned projects. A product breakdown structure (PBS) aids understanding of the WBS. It focuses on the product of the project, breaking it into smaller and smaller components. It could be considered a *pro forma* engineering bill of materials.

Consider an automobile. It might be described as consisting of a chassis and power train. The power train can be broken down into engine, transmission, and wheels and the wheels into brakes, axle, bearings, rims, tires, and so forth. Some of the identified components may be carried over from a previous model; thus, the work content on such components is nominal. On the other hand, designing a new engine requires considerable time and a large work content.

For a manufacturing plant, one of the outputs of process engineering is a manufacturing bill of materials, comparable to a PBS. In an information systems project, the PBS consists of the structured programming diagram and, if it includes hardware procurement or different use of hardware, may include those components of the system. In both of these examples, use of existing components reduces the work content of the project, leading to fewer required resources, earlier project completion, and fewer problems.

Having a well-defined PBS leads to a well-developed WBS, providing the basis for effective delegation.

Minimize Changes

Preplanning, as described in the previous section, will aid in minimizing changes during the execution phase of the project.

It is the basic irony of projects that while a project is the means for creating change, change in the project is one of the most prevalent sources of problems in executing the project. This is a justification of the famous maxim on bidding projects: bid low and make it up on changes.

As tempting as this may be, changes often lead to errors, rework, further changes, delay, and reduced productivity. The first four of these should be obvious; reduced productivity may need some clarification.

Perhaps you've had the experience of painting a room in your house while your spouse was away for a day or two. Your spouse returns and shares a few negative comments about the color you chose and insists that you repaint. Would you be as enthusiastic and productive while redoing this project? Not likely. A request for a third redo would probably lead to harsh words and a sloppy job at best.

Is it possible that your project team members might feel the same way? Some project managers may conclude that this should not matter to members as long as they get paid for all of the work. This may be true in the mechanical view of people, but it will destroy sense of ownership and pride in the project, and you may well get a *sloppy job* in return.

Changes are expensive. On one project, it was judged that a one-month delay in the issuing of the bid package would lead to another $5,000,000 worth of work being defined. It was estimated that work not included in the bid package would have to be incorporated into the project by change orders at a 20 percent increase in costs. The delay was authorized, and $1,000,000 was saved.

Estimate and Negotiate for Resources

Estimating is much more than throwing darts or gazing into a glass sphere. It requires knowing the nature of the organization, the project team members, ambient weather, labor, and other conditions, and a host of other variables. It also requires an honest evaluation of your leadership capabilities.

The concept of *discretionary effort* is discussed in *The World's Greatest Project* (Darnall 1996). If you as project manager are effective in all the skill areas described, you may be able to create a high-energy team that sets performance records. Failure to plan effectively, anticipate problems, or get ahead of the wave—resulting in your team always waiting on you—can lead to excessive time required to perform those same tasks.

Furthermore, you must realize that your project is only one of many in process in your organization or community. The resources you need most may be needed on one or more other projects. Your success in getting the best resources will depend on your ability to negotiate. Sometimes you will have to negotiate with higher management to gain its recognition and commitment to your project. Sometimes you will have to directly negotiate with the resource. Price is not necessarily the primary variable. Often your ability to schedule effectively and perform to that schedule will be critical in these negotiations. Consider the point of view of the drywall contractor who arrives at the job site to find that the job has not progressed as scheduled. If he moves to the next job, it may be weeks before you are back on his schedule.

Schedule Multidisciplinary Activities

The first project that you manage will likely be *monodisciplinary*, meaning that you will do the whole thing. If you prove that you can manage the single-resource project—that is, by yourself—the next one may involve two resources, and then three, and so on. Start from the beginning, using accepted practices. Become skilled in each aspect of project management as you go, as these skills will be far more valuable as the number of zeros in your project budget grows.

An aside to those who establish standard practices in organizations: The above should be recognized when establishing standard practices. Some organizations manage small projects in a different manner than large projects. Sometimes there are even more than two methodologies. It is argued here that all such methodologies should be consistent as they apply to larger and larger projects. Lessons learned on small projects should be applicable to larger projects. Smaller projects should simply require a subset of the methodology for larger projects. This will enhance skill development and keep relearning costs to a minimum.

Plan and Organize Multifunctional Programs

As you progress, managing larger and larger projects, there will be a discontinuity as you become responsible for multiple projects—i.e., a program. A program may be simply a set of projects aimed toward achieving a single objective, such as creating all the facilities necessary to produce a new product. If you are in an element of the United States Department of Defense as a program manager, you likely will be responsible for the development, production, deployment, logistical support, and decommissioning of a new weapons system. Probably the most significant change in your life will be the degree to which you will be involved in the politics of projects, both internally and externally. Of course, if you were lucky on the way to this *opportunity*, you will have been involved in projects having political facets.

Measure

"If you can't measure it, you can't control it." How often have you heard that maxim? Conversely, if you measure it, you may not have to control it—but only if you monitor it. The fact that you are measuring it will make those responsible more conscious of what is really happening and what should be happening.

The Type 1 error is to measure too many things, the most likely behavior of the beginning project manager. If in doubt, measure it; however, there is a cost. Measuring too many things results in a reduction of productivity.

The Type 2 error is failing to measure a critical variable. As a result, you are unaware of a pending problem until it is already nipping you.

Probably the best advice for the project manager is to manage by walking around. The best project scheduling and control system measures only some of what is really happening on the project, and that information will probably become visible late. The effective project manager has antennae deployed in many directions. To be an effective project manager, you must take advantage of both the formal and informal information systems.

This OC's early experience led to anxiety that something would go wrong on the project. It did—but it wasn't a catastrophe. Soon his attitude changed to: "Something is going to go wrong. I wonder if I can discover it and fix it before anybody else becomes aware of it." To a large extent, this was achieved via managing by walking around. Get on your feet and out of your office. You will be surprised by what you learn. Listen to what people tell you, but test and verify it before you act.

Work Status, Progress, and Performance

This may truly be the most difficult part of managing a project. In your early stages of development as a project manager, you will be inclined to spend too much time managing the technology. You must allocate time to analyze the reports that you receive and talk with members of your project team. It is the dynamics of this process that really lead you to understanding what is happening on your project. Failure to do it will convey the message that reports and progress are not really important. Similarly, failure to keep your boss and the client informed inevitably leads to surprises. Do you like surprises? Surprises are great for birthdays and April Fools' Day; surprises in business can be disastrous to your project, boss, client, and yourself.

It is tempting to fudge reports to show that the project is on time and on budget. This is one way to avoid the extra *help* that often comes from above when the project gets off track. On the other hand, honest, forthright progress reporting will instill confidence that you know what is going on and will keep others properly informed. Better yet, if there is a decision to be made, provide alternatives with well-done staff work to facilitate decision-making.

SUMMARY

In the last three chapters, we have discussed the three primary skill areas of the project manager: leadership, technology, and administration. It is quite a challenge to develop all of them. The good news is that these skills do not have to be developed all at once. The bad news is that these last three chapters have simply introduced you to the subjects.

In this chapter, we discussed some key administrative skills. The last three skills require knowledge of basic project planning, scheduling, and control. (They will be the main thrust of the chapters that follow, as well as in *PM 102*.)

Just as in sports an excellent performer must have the basics down pat, it is not enough to learn the basics and never return to them again. Constant drill and practice are required. Also, as in sports, failures can more often than not be traced back to failure on the fundamentals.

> This session provided some insights that made Sam feel confident that the raft was indeed a "possible dream." It was apparent that communicating effectively is important, as it was included in all

three of the skill areas. It was also clear that interpersonal skills were important—in this case to attract and hold capable people and delegate effectively. Understanding policies and procedures was new to Sam. His only experience to date had been claiming reimbursement of expenses. The Great Guru stressed some new stuff like minimizing changes, estimating resources required, scheduling multidisciplinary activities, planning and organizing multifunctional programs, measuring progress, and reporting work status and performance.

Sam was a bit overwhelmed by these visits to the Great Temples. After all, these three gurus had prescribed a great deal of learning. Sam had doubts about this challenge. Returning home, he passed the Temple of the leadership guru and heard a voice from atop the peak: **"There are technological, administrative, and leadership skills, and the greatest of these is leadership! Find yourself a mentor who is a leader. Find a project manager who has been up and down the trail many times, and heed that project manager's advice."**

Sam was determined to follow these last instructions; but first there were some specific skills that needed sharpening. Sam wandered off and sat under a large shade tree and reflected on this newfound wisdom, wondering where a workshop on these skills could be found.

"Call PMI!" came a loud whisper from above. Sam, being very professional and a recognized self-starter, vowed to improve the rest of these skills.

APPENDIX VI.A— MARS PATHFINDER PROJECT

The Mars Pathfinder Project had many different audiences with which it communicated:

1. Jet Propulsion Laboratory (JPL) Internal Audience—Since Pathfinder was a very important and high-visibility mission for National Aeronautics and Space Administration (NASA), JPL senior management was very interested in the status along the way. There was also much interest among other JPL employees.

2. NASA—The Office of Space Science had programmatic responsibility for the project at NASA Headquarters.
3. Science Community—Many scientists studying Mars and the solar system had a professional interest in utilizing the science data that was acquired.
4. Schools (educators and students)—Many teachers in the technical disciplines had a strong interest in motivating their students by exposing them to the space program and the study of the planets.
5. General Public—The public at large has always been fascinated by space exploration and the planet Mars in particular.
6. Private Industry—Interested in new technologies and possible spin-offs from the Mars Pathfinder Mission.

A variety of approaches were required in order to effectively reach these audiences.

JPL senior management was briefed on a monthly basis in the JPL director's review meeting about the technical and programmatic project status. The Pathfinder team was also proactive in doing presentations about the status of the project for the benefit of the JPL employees.

The team was in constant communication with NASA about the status of the project. This was accomplished through the NASA monthly management review process, quarterly reviews, annual operating plan review, and numerous peer reviews. The Pathfinder management staff would also keep in touch with its NASA counterparts on a regular basis by telephone and email.

The Pathfinder project scientist kept the outside science community informed and involved throughout the entire project by holding open science workshops and publishing numerous abstracts and papers in respected science journals. For example, two open science workshops were held during the Pathfinder landing site-selection process.

The Pathfinder team has been heavily involved with an extensive education and public outreach program from the beginning of the project. Project members have helped create educational modules for use in public schools and partnered with high schools and colleges to participate in mentoring programs. The project produced a variety of educational and public outreach materials that have been distributed to schools and the general public. In addition, Pathfinder team members have spent hundreds of hours doing presentations to schools and civic organizations all around the country, as well as assisting with hundreds of tour groups that have visited JPL during the project. The project has also worked hard to communicate with industry regarding the technological advances that have occurred on the project, as part of our commitment to technology transfer.

Two other very important parts of our successful communications management program have been the development of our Internet website, and our public information campaign during landing day and surface operations.

An extensive website was developed, which allowed updating of project information to internal and external audiences. During the seven-month cruise to Mars, we worked on building up our website capabilities for the anticipated demand on landing day. Over thirty mirror sites were established worldwide, allowing tens of millions of people all over the world to access images and information on Pathfinder landing in near real time. At last count, we had over 735 million hits on our Pathfinder websites.

Project management in conjunction with the JPL Public Information Office conceived the public information campaign. This was a major challenge: trying to accommodate the hundreds of news media at JPL during landing week while keeping the team focused on the mission. By setting up cameras in Pathfinder mission control with a feed to NASA TV, all major television news organizations could access the drama in real time during the landing event, allowing millions of people all over the world to view the event live. This was a primary reason that the Pathfinder mission was such a public relations success. The Pathfinder project did an excellent job of *humanizing* the mission for the public. For example, naming the Martian rocks after familiar public characters allowed people to follow and participate more in the event.

Chapter VII

Scope Management

RENDER UNTO THY CLIENT THAT
FOR WHICH THY CLIENT HAS AGREED TO PAY.

Sam reflected on the characteristics of a project manager and took some immediate action. Realizing that the objectives of the project may not be clear, Sam went to the client. After considerable probing, it was determined that the client intended to move across the river. A raft was needed to carry the family, all the household items, fifty sheepskins of grain, thirty sheep, twenty geese, ten goats, five asses, two oxen, and one aged mother-in-law. Sam pondered these requirements and their implications on the specifications for the raft.

From this information, Sam was able to visualize the raft. It would be made of logs, held together by strips of leather, and tied to an upstream tree with grapevines.

Sam began to feel better about this stuff called "project management." While the demands of being a project manager were great, they did not seem out of reach. It was now time to get on with the details of how to get the raft built. Sam recalled two admonitions from earlier lessons: "Render unto thy client that for which thy client has agreed to pay," and "Thou shalt knowest what thou was asked to create."

Somehow this seems so simple, but could it really be? Could there be more to it than meets the eye? Are there traps and pitfalls ahead?

Projects come in all shapes and sizes and can be either internal (in-house) or external to the project manager's organization. While the following discussion implies an external project of some magnitude, the concepts are applicable to a project of any magnitude, as well as to internal projects. Simply read client as boss and contractor as myself.

Projects are different from most repetitive productive efforts. It might be possible to "lose a little on each unit but make it up on volume" on the repetitive efforts. It won't work on projects, as they are only done once. Thus, if you don't make a profit on almost every one, you will soon be out of business. The first step is to get a clear statement of objectives of the client.

Ideally, the client has a clear understanding, as evident in Appendix VII-A, Mission Objective and Project Requirements for the Mars Pathfinder Project. (Note: The mission was originally referred to as the MESUR Pathfinder Project.) This was the statement of requirements developed jointly by NASA and the Jet Propulsion Laboratory (JPL). Much of the success of this project started with this statement. The project team had a clear understanding of what was required and the limits within which the project was to be performed. In fairness, it should be noted that this statement was written as a cooperative effort between the client and the project team, not at all an unusual process.

Another example of a clear understanding of the requirements was evident in a project to construct a plant for a pharmaceutical company. Its needs were stated something like the following: "We want a plant in Puerto Rico that meets all applicable FDA and other United States government regulations, and that will house an operation to produce a specific quantity of pills per year of a new pharmaceutical that is expected to have a product life of just five years. The market is ready for this product now! We do not anticipate a use for this facility beyond this." This description gives a clear idea of what this project is all about. First, it describes what has to be housed, where, and for what capacity. It challenges the designers to create a general-purpose facility that would have value in an alternative use in five years. It says that, while a low-cost design is relevant, cost is much less important than getting into production as soon as possible (ASAP).

The client will not always have such a clear understanding, particularly on in-house projects. For example, following an executive meeting at which it was decided that Chrysler would introduce a 5/50-warranty program, the Corporate Systems Department was notified "to develop an information system to administer this program." A feasibility study was launched that identified eight system alternatives. Even after the preferred alternative was selected and the project was well under way, there were many changes in the requirements. Perhaps the most significant changes were the introduction of a new computer mass-storage device and a new and significantly improved computer, both of which afforded the opportunity to reach management's objectives to a greater degree than was possible at the start of the project.

A more vivid example can be imagined for the project manager of the restoration of I-580 following the earthquake in the San Francisco area in 1989. Imagine being called into your boss' office the morning after this disaster and being told, "Effective immediately, you are the project manager. Our office in Oakland will provide you space and personnel as required. Now get hopping!" That really happened, and the person assigned that job had to decide what to do first. Clearly, the first priority was to rescue anyone trapped, and the second was to prevent any further injury or damage from occurring. Only after attending to those tasks was this individual able to start thinking about the overall requirements for the project.

When the objectives, requirements, and desires are not clear in the beginning, the project manager must restate the requirements in specific, unambiguous terms and obtain acceptance of these requirements by the client. Some of these requirements will pertain to the product of the project. Other requirements will pertain to the project itself, focusing on schedule, cost, quality, and risk.

The most important of these requirements will be the terms of acceptance of the completed product of the project. It can be very detrimental to a project manager's career to complete the project only to have the client say, "That's not what I wanted!" Only after these requirements are clearly stated and agreed to can the plans for the project be developed with assurance that the client will be satisfied with the final result.

Project managers have often been impetuous, claiming that they have no time to plan the project because they have to get on with the technical work of the project. Sometimes the project may be so critical to corporate strategy that action must be initiated without a clear statement of requirements. In such instances, it may be advisable to get some action started ASAP. This may be especially true for safety and security matters, long lead-time items, or items for which it is known that vendor capacity may be limited. For example, a systems project required several computers at a time when they were "on allocation." An early commitment was made with the vendor to secure a position in the allocation process long before the system design was completed. However, such urgency is no excuse for allowing the project to progress too far before nailing the requirements for both the product of the project and the project.

On the other hand, you must be realistic in accepting the fact that requirements are seldom cast in concrete—bronze perhaps, but not concrete; bronze can be reshaped far more easily than concrete.

At a Project Management Institute chapter meeting, a simple solution was offered for avoiding after-the-fact disputes and their associated costs: write a better contract with a more complete statement of work! Later, a rhetorical question was asked: "Have you ever performed a project exactly as called for in the contract?" One person raised a hand. When "100 percent?" was added, the hand slowly went down. Of course, that was expected. It is in the nature of projects that there will be change.

The anomaly of projects is that while projects are to create change, change itself creates most of the problems of managing projects.

THE GENESIS OF PROJECTS

Projects are initiated as the result of a perceived need. The need may be to expand capacity to produce an existing product. The need may be for a structure to house people or objects. The need may be for a new product or service for which a market is deemed to exist. The product must be designed and tested and facilities prepared for its manufacture.

Whatever the need, there is an urgency to fulfill it. The urgency leads to two things: a pressure to get on with the project, and less than complete knowledge of what is actually required. In addition, there is an inevitable pressure to complete the project without spending any more money than is necessary, given the urgency and the performance requirements for the product of the project. Perceptions differ on how much money is *necessary*.

Under such conditions, there is inevitably risk. Risk that the project duration will be longer than expected. Risk that the cost will exceed expectations. Risk that society will insist on requirements being met that were never anticipated. Risk that the performance of the product of the project will be less than was expected. And, yes, risk that the need for the product of the project will disappear—e.g., the Edsel and the Superconducting Super Collider—or that a competitor will meet the need first and thus significantly reduce your market share. All of these risks must be weighed in decision-making about the project.

Therefore, the instigator of a project must make a myriad of decisions in the face of less than complete information. If the contract is desired, the contractor who hopes to provide the services of performing the project must also make many decisions in the face of less than complete information. Hence, the game is defined.

There have been times—and with certain people—when agreements to perform a project could be based on a handshake. That happens occasionally even today. However, the pressure for profits and the litigious nature of our society make it extremely questionable. So it is common practice to enter into contracts to define the relationships between two parties to a project and the nature of the product that is to be produced. This is appropriate even on most in-house projects.

Characteristically, the contract-development process has been a complex game to define the product desired by the client and the project that is to be performed to produce that product. The client is motivated to obtain the product at the least cost, time, and risk while the contractor is motivated to get the project, make a profit, and accept minimum risk. The stage is set for conflict!

It could be argued that both parties are acting in good faith—the client not wanting anything for which he has not paid a fair price, and the contractor dedicated to deliver everything for which payment is received. But that would lead to a rather short and uninteresting, if not unrealistic, analysis. The more likely scenario is that each party is looking out for its own self-interests, generally in the short run. (For an alternative to this game, see the section, Minimizing Disputes, in this chapter.)

Given this scenario, it is easy to impute all sorts of behaviors to both the client and the contractor. For example, one strategy sometimes followed by contractors is to bid low and make it up on changes. The client may use a strategy of omitting some of the small details, expecting to persuade the contractor to do them without issuing change orders. So what can be done to manage this game?

The first step is to establish a clear definition of what is understood to be the product of the project and what work will be done to produce that product. This presumes a relatively clear idea of the nature of the product of the project and the work required to produce it. This understanding must be put in writing in a clear and concise manner. It forms the baseline from which future changes in the product, the project, or both can be measured.

Often it is necessary to describe the product in terms of performance requirements. In such cases, it is much more difficult to describe accurately the work content of the project, especially when the project involves pushing the state of the art of one or more technologies. This makes defining the baseline more difficult. Nevertheless, the more definitive the baseline, the less likelihood there is for disagreement during the project, especially at the end of the project.

In the discussion of project scope management in *A Guide to the Project Management Body of Knowledge* (PMBOK® Guide), a clear distinction is made between "product scope" and "project scope." They are defined in the *PMBOK® Guide* as follows:

> Product scope—the features and functions that are to be included in a product or service.

> Project scope—the work that must be done in order to deliver a product with the specified features and functions.

The *PMBOK® Guide* goes on to say that "the processes, tools, and techniques used to manage product scope vary by application area and are usually defined as part of the project life cycle."

Both product scope and project scope require the attention of the project manager. Following is a discussion of each.

MANAGING PRODUCT SCOPE

The first step in defining product scope is to clearly identify the deliverables. Perhaps we want a house with three thousand square feet of floor area on three floor levels (basement, first, and second) with ten rooms and a three-car garage.

Then we must decide just how many services and what degree of completion we expect for the house. For example, a project to build a house could include only the construction necessary to obtain an occupancy permit. The design might be off the shelf. You might choose to purchase all the style items—e.g., lighting, plumbing fixtures, special doors, and so on. You might do the decorating and landscaping. On the other hand, if you are about to return from a foreign assignment to your company's home office in a very demanding position, you might decide to award a single turnkey contract for designing, building, decorating, and landscaping. The cost of the house will be substantially different for each approach, as will the time until project completion and the work content for the owner.

Consider just the house. The next step would be to develop a product breakdown structure (PBS). Some of the items that might be included are: exterior, interior, utilities, HVAC, and spaces. Each of these could then be subdivided. Thus, a partial PBS might appear as in Figure VII.1.

Under each of these items, additional detail would be added in each case to remove ambiguity. From this simple example, it is easier to see the concept of progressive elaboration taking place, a concept that is inherent in projects.

In addition to the physical features identified in Table VII.1, there are some other criteria that should be considered, as described in Table VII.2. The term *ilities* refers to a number of criteria, all of which end in *ility*, such as usability and maintainability. Examples are suggested, based on the house project, to illustrate the concepts. The characteristics should be tailored to the products as appropriate. The use of the word "Echelon" is familiar to anyone who has been in military service, where it is used to categorize the skills and facilities required for different maintenance tasks and who is to perform them. It is used here in the same sense. The meaning of the various echelons should be modified to be applicable to the specific product.

The priorities assigned to these may vary between individuals and organizations. One way to clarify the priorities is to rate them as:

1. Essential—must be present in product.

2. Desirable—would add utility/benefits but could be sacrificed.

3. Nice to have—would add some utility/benefits but not willing to pay much for it.

4. Of no value—adds no utility/benefits.

These priorities should be modified to meet the needs of the particular project.

Associated with this process, you might want to make estimates of the costs of each item and exercise a concept often referred to as design cost control. If cost is of no concern, this could be omitted. If it is a design-to-maximum-cost project, this is essential.

For example, suppose the project were to design a new food processor that might appear in the kitchen of the house. The consumer expectations as expressed in the marketplace and the competitive offerings combine to define price/function/feature categories. You may have selected a specific range of these categories in which to compete. Thus, there is a maximum suggested retail price, less retailer markup, less distribution

General
    Floor area
    Floor levels
    Garages

Exterior
    Overall style
    Siding
    Roof
    Windows
    Entries

Interior
    Overall style
    Floor plan
        Basement
        First floor
        Second floor
    Wall finish (plaster, sheet rock, etc.)
    Flooring

Spaces
    Living room
    Dining room
    Family room
    Kitchen
        Cabinets
        Appliances
        Plumbing fixtures
    Detail floor plan
        Bedrooms
        Bathrooms

Utilities
    Electric
    Water
        Treatment
        Heating
    Sewer

HVAC
    Passive Solar
    Finnish wood heater or equivalent
    Heat pump
    Insulation
    Fans

Electronics
    Entry signals and control
    Intercom system
    Telephone system
    Stereo with multiple speakers
    Television reception and outlets
    Computer ports (LANS)

TABLE VII.1

A Partial Product Breakdown Structure of Physical Features and Functions

costs, and less manufacturer markup, which defines the maximum cost content of the product. By pricing the components, the work content to assemble the product, packaging, user manual, and warranty costs, you can assess whether the product design is economically viable or not. At

Security—protection from outside threats
- ❑ Protection of occupants and possessions from physical entry.
- ❑ Protection of valuables in the event of physical entry.

Safety—protection from inside threats
- ❑ Prevention of accidents such as tripping on carpets or uneven floors, or exposure to electrical shock.
- ❑ Prevention of fires through physical separation of spaces; special facilities for storing combustibles, alarm systems, and extinguishing systems.

Environmental Friendliness—the degree to which the product impinges on the environment
- ❑ Solar heating and adequate insulation consumes less energy.
- ❑ Waste-disposal facilities encourage proper disposal of recyclable and hazardous materials.

Performance—the *ilities*
Usability: the ability of the typical user to use the item for normally intended uses; often called *user friendliness*
- ❑ Many people can relate to this with personal computers; the OC also finds it very applicable to home entertainment centers. Human engineering can add greatly to usability by placement and design of controls, for example.

Availability: the percentage of time that the unit is available for intended uses. This is often described by *mean time to failure* or similar measures
- ❑ The OC has one component of the home entertainment center, a multiple speaker control, which has failed three times in some ten years and has had to be sent to the factory for repair. Only one pair of speakers was available while it was out.

Repairability: the ability to access the item to make repairs and the (inverse of) degree of expertise required to perform repairs
- ❑ Some products are placed in positions that require extensive effort to access. For example, replacing the clutch on some cars requires pulling the engine.
- ❑ Some products simply are not repairable; others require special tools; and some have simple pluggable items that can be easily replaced.

TABLE VII.2

Product Design Characteristics—*Continued on next page*

Maintainability: the relative ease of keeping the item in good operating
condition and appearance

Echelon	Frequency	By
1st	daily	user

❏ Ease of cleaning kitchen counters and floors varies, depending on the materials used and the layout.

2nd	weekly	user

❏ Lawn maintenance can be made easier by minimizing the hand trimming.

3rd	monthly	user

❏ Washing windows can be made easier by selecting windows that make access to the exterior side easy.

4th	seasonally/annual	user

❏ Preparation for seasonal requirements, such as freezing weather, can be made easier by using proper materials and design.

5th	as needed	user/contractor

❏ Roof repairs and painting can be minimized by the selection of proper materials.

TABLE VII.2

Continued

that point, value engineering and other techniques can be applied to attempt to reduce the costs without sacrificing any of the functions or features. Throughout this process, careful attention must be paid to the ability of the product to provide the necessary customer satisfaction when the product is introduced in the market.

On many products of projects, it is important to maintain an accurate record of the components of the product. This is normally referred to as configuration management. One type of product makes this concept very vivid. In developing a very large computer system, composed of many modules of coding, each module will be thoroughly tested before it is integrated into the system. If a change is made in an already approved module, it is no longer the same component. It must be tested to ensure that the change did not introduce an unintended consequence. Until it has been thoroughly tested, it should not be introduced into the system. Configuration management identifies exactly what components have been introduced and provides verification of its test results.

Now consider the implications of that software being installed on a space vehicle. We have read of instances where, when a problem occurs, a troubleshooting effort is initiated here on Earth. This often involves simulating the conditions on the space vehicle, using the same code that is on board. If the system has not had careful configuration management to ensure that the code being used in simulation is exactly the same as on the space vehicle, the results are unreliable.

Similarly, all physical components must be controlled through configuration management. This typically includes not only identification such as a serial number, but also test results for the component and the exact date of production of the part and all of its components. If it is a metal part, it should be possible to trace it back to a particular pour of that metal and the metallurgical tests that were run on that batch.

> If you don't know where you are going, how will you know when you get there?
>
> *Alice in Wonderland*

MANAGING PROJECT SCOPE

The *PMBOK® Guide* discusses the management of project scope in terms of five distinct processes: 1) initiation, 2) scope planning, 3) scope definition, 4) scope verification, and 5) scope change control.

Project Initiation

In the discussion of the genesis of a project, we stated that "projects are initiated as the result of a perceived need." The key words are "need" and "perceived." It is unlikely that a project will be started unless there is a need for the product of the project. It may spring from a strategic analysis of an organization, be it a market need, a military weapons system need, a need for a disease cure, or even the need for a change of scenery at home. The need may be latent until someone perceives it. In an organization, top management may perceive it, or it can rise from the ranks through something like a quality circle. Generally, in the latter instance, it is necessary to persuade higher-level management to allocate the resources; however, as has been experienced in quality circles, there may be an implicit authorization to proceed under certain conditions. Sometimes projects are bootlegged into an organization by using up any resources remaining from other authorized projects.

Projects can be initiated at various stages in the process of creating the product to fulfill the need. Customarily, a project to build a house starts with a lot of research by the person(s) perceiving the need. They may select a parcel of land, using the assistance of a realtor, or purchase the lot and house through a development. They may hire an architect to draw plans, or they may select an off-the-shelf design. They might even select a manufactured home or a motor home. (The OC has experience with this latter option.) The architect's services may be used to get bids and select a builder, and may include overseeing the project until the occupancy permit is received. On the other hand, the owner may act as the builder, doing almost all the work, or act as general contractor, hiring the individual subcontractors. (The OC has experience with this, too.) Most projects have this same sort of variability in initiation.

The outputs from the initiation process are a project charter, the identification or assignment of a project manager, and a statement of constraints and assumptions. The project charter contains the authorization "to apply an organization's resources to project activities." It should also contain a clear statement as to exactly what authority is assigned. For example, does the project manager have control of all funds, releasing them only upon agreement with a functional manager on what will be done when and for what cost? Does the project manager have authority to purchase goods and services, or must all that go through purchasing? Once the charter is published, it will be difficult to obtain further authorizations and probably more difficult to achieve actual recognition of the new authority by others without creating more of a stir than many project managers desire.

Scope Planning

"Scope planning is the process of developing a written scope statement as the basis for future project decisions including, in particular, the criteria used to determine if the project or phase has been completed successfully" (*PMBOK® Guide*). Outputs from this process include a scope statement, supporting detail, and a scope management plan.

Contents of the scope statement should include project justification, project product description, project deliverables, and project objectives. Supporting detail includes any other documents that may be needed during executing the project. The scope management plan details the steps that will be taken to ensure that all deliverables are completed, all the work is performed satisfactorily, and no changes are made to the project scope without formal recognition and consideration of costs.

Scope Definition

Using the above, and any other information that may be relevant, the next step is to subdivide the total project into *doable* work packages, which can be assigned to an individual or an organizational element. The output from this effort is the work breakdown structure (WBS), which is so important to the orderly progress of a project that it is discussed separately in Chapter VIII.

Some of the advantages of using a WBS are cited in the *PMBOK®
Guide*:
❑ "Improve the accuracy of cost, time, and resource estimates."
❑ "Define a baseline for performance measurement and control."
❑ "Facilitate clear responsibility assignment."

The WBS clearly establishes the work that must be done to perform the project and therefore determines the work content of the project. The project manager's task is to ensure that all the work content is done in the most efficient manner, resulting in completing all deliverables at the least cost. To a large extent this is accomplished by motivating those who are actually performing the work.

In defining the project through the WBS, the same or a similar method of establishing priorities should be used as discussed under the PBS. There are tasks that have to be performed; i.e., they are essential. There are some that are desirable in that they give added assurance that the product of the project will meet all the client's objectives. For example, a new component might be tested to destruction to determine its behavior through its entire life cycle. On the other hand, it might be decided to use a proven component instead, to overdesign the item to essentially preclude failure, or that the likely use of the product will not exhaust the useful life of the item. There are some tasks that would be nice, but it is understood that the client might not want to pay for them. For example, these might be public-relations events that are of primary benefit to the performing organization. There may be some things that the client just does not want done associated with this project. The project manager and the project team should have a clear understanding of these priorities. (See Figure VII.1 for an example of a form for documenting a work package.)

Scope Verification

Scope verification is the process of formalizing acceptance of the product(s) of the project. It includes ensuring that all aspects of the product scope are achieved and all the work of the project scope has been performed. The more thoroughly this process is performed, the less likely there will be delays in closing out the project as it winds down. One way to minimize problems at the end is to provide the client with interim reports and demonstrations as each phase of the project is completed and each deliverable is tendered.

Scope Change Control
(or Dealing with Sneaky, Creepy Change)

If change is inevitable in projects, we must behave as if it will happen rather than as if it will not happen. Working from this understanding, it is reasonable to manage the changes in such a way as to build confidence between the parties to the contract and protect the financial

Date: _____

	Number	Description	Manager	Organization
WBS	_____	_____	_____	_____
WP	_____	_____	_____	_____

Scope of Work:

_____
_____
_____
_____
_____
_____
_____

Comments/Constraints:

_____
_____
_____

Cost and Schedule

	NEGOTIATED					ACTUALS			
Activity	Start	Complete	Labor Hrs.	DC ($)		Start	Complete	Labor Hrs.	DC ($)
1. _____	___	_____	___	___		___	_____	___	___
2. _____	___	_____	___	___		___	_____	___	___
3. _____	___	_____	___	___		___	_____	___	___
4. _____	___	_____	___	___		___	_____	___	___
5. _____	___	_____	___	___		___	_____	___	___

Functional Manager	Date	WBS Manager	Date
_____	____	_____	____

WP Manager	Date	Project Manager	Date
_____	____	_____	____

Source: Work Agreements: The Process for Getting Project Work Done, Sandia National Laboratories, Albuquerque, New Mexico, December 1991, p. 11.

FIGURE VII.1

An Example of a Form for Defining a Work Package

interests of both parties. There are two aspects of change that require managing: formal and informal.

Formal change is the most straightforward to manage. Basically, there is a recognition that the product of the project must be different from what was originally envisaged, or that a process of the project must be modified to meet other client needs. Either the client or the contractor may recognize the need for change. A formal request is issued, the impact of the change is analyzed, the cost is estimated, and the price is submitted to the client. The client either accepts, rejects, or negotiates—eventually making a deal. Managing this process requires excellent administrative procedures combined with very fast resolution of the issue. Failure to achieve speedy resolution often leads to dispute, either about delays or the acceptable cost of the change.

One essential aspect of change management is document control. Since change is inevitable, the effective and assured communication of all changes is of the utmost importance. All members of the team must be playing from the same sheet of music. The result if this is not done can be interesting. For example, in building a house, the plumber was not provided the latest drawing. A drainpipe from the upstairs sink ended up cast in concrete about six inches from the changed location of the partition in which it was to run. Upon completion of the house, a small white ceramic vessel was installed on that partition and connected to the drain line. The result was the availability of an unexpected convenience item in the garage/workshop.

Informal change is the difficult part to manage; it is insidious. Without a clearly defined baseline for scope, it may be impossible to identify the change.

One scenario in developing a computer-based system is for the client to sit with the programmer and suggest modifications to the program that go beyond the specifications. "Wouldn't it be neat if we just add three more lines of code?" is typical. Being an ingenious and obliging programmer, the statements are added. Not being in the specifications, there is no test for them. Eventually, they show up in the last integration test, causing test failure, much searching for the problem, and rework to remove the offending statements. Sometimes the code works, and the client gets a nice freebie. To paraphrase the late Senator

Everett Dirksen: "A small change here, a small change there, and the first thing you know you are talking real money."

What can be done to manage informal change? A well-disciplined project team is important. Even more effective is a team that is motivated by incentives tied to successful completion of the project. Management may say, "But those incentives cut into our profit!" On the other hand, the cost of rework, delays in completing the project and receiving payment, and resolving disputes may completely wipe out all profit—and more.

For the internal project, it is equally, if not more, important to document scope. Bosses are often even more adept at changing the scope of work. Formal change can be managed as discussed earlier. Documentation is the key. Informal change may require more adroit behaviors. For example, one boss used to have the OC write speeches for him. The number of these requests kept increasing (analogous to scope creep). After one such speech was written and approved by the boss, the OC was asked to get it approved by corporate public relations, who asked that one paragraph be modified to reflect a positive rather than negative view. It was easy but required the use of the phrase, "all other things being equal," or its Latin counterpart, ceteris paribus. After careful calculations, the probability that the boss would reread the speech before getting to the podium was determined to be nil. The OC used ceteris paribus. The boss stared at those words for, well, quite a while. Thereafter, the OC's scope of work, in terms of writing speeches, was somewhat reduced. This is not a generally recommended strategy except for the most job-secure or the most foolhardy.

PROJECT LIFE CYCLES

Some projects inherently involve a high degree of uncertainty. This is particularly true in innovative efforts such as developing totally new products. Clients sometimes are unsure of the exact requirements. Often there is uncertainty about the results of development efforts. For example, the process of developing a new pharmaceutical requires a series of tests to ensure its efficacy and safety. Developing a new military weapons system often requires the development of new technology that must be tested and proven before it is used in the system.

One way to deal with this situation is to break the project down into phases, with each phase designed to reduce the uncertainties in the next phase. Go/no-go decisions at the end of each phase provide a means of controlling the commitments for the future. An excellent way to manage the scope of a project is to design critical reviews at the end of each phase of the life cycle. An example of this can be seen in Paragraph 2.3.3 in Appendix VIII.A. Each milestone represents the end of a significant phase of the project. If any problems are discovered at the reviews, they should be corrected before committing resources to the next phase.

There are several guidelines for establishing phases in a project. One approach is to look for points of transition of responsibility. For example, when the responsibility shifts from one contractor to another, a review of the work of the first contractor can ensure that all work has been completed in accordance with specifications. Once the next contractor moves onto the job, the first contractor will have a plethora of excuses for not being responsible. On a construction project, inspections are scheduled to minimize the chances of tearing out subsequent work to correct an unsatisfactory condition in previous work. Thus, underground utilities are inspected before foundations and floors are poured. Another approach is to identify major areas of uncertainty to ensure that the remaining uncertainty has been minimized before allowing further work to proceed. This is particularly important if some of the components of the project are pushing the state of the art of the relevant technology. This is often the case on defense systems acquisitions and the development of new pharmaceuticals. Similarly, there are natural review points just before major expenditures commence. Thus, a review of laboratory production results for a new chemical compound should precede authorization of construction of a pilot plant. Similarly, a review of pilot plant results should precede authorization of construction of full-scale production facilities.

MINIMIZING DISPUTES

One of the hazards of engaging in project-type work is the prevalence of disputes. Some companies have literally gone out of business as a result of intransigent clients insisting on restitution for damages alleged as a result of a project that went sour. Many—if not most—disputes can be traced directly to inadequate scope management. Good scope management can minimize the chances of such disputes. There are other approaches that assist in avoiding disputes.

Partnering

One of the interesting areas of project management today is the quest for better ways of working together to minimize, if not remove, conflict. Many organizations have engaged in a practice commonly called partnering. (Partnering was the focus of the September 1994 issue of *PM Network*.) In partnering, the basic approach is to change the game from *me versus them* to *we*. One way to view the situation is that the client has temporarily hired the contractor's personnel for the duration. If the project comes out well, the client may hire the personnel again. If the project is approached with both parties on the same side, their respective self-interests are best served by selecting the ultimate best solution for the client. This does not negate the need for scope management but does make it somewhat easier, because a change affects both parties in the same manner.

Alternate Dispute Resolution

Under this approach, the parties to a project agree up-front to resolve disputes in an expeditious manner, relying on mediators or arbitrators if necessary. This has reduced the total cost of disputes, as well as reduced the time lost waiting for a decision. (For more on this subject, consider reading the earlier-mentioned articles in the September 1994 *PM Network*.)

THE GOOD NEWS

Avoiding disputes is only one benefit of good scope management. It leads to greater profitability, more repeat business, and probably more new business. It leads to greater satisfaction by the project team and greater willingness on the part of good team members to want to be on the project manager's team in the future. It also leads to more peaceful sleep and lower bills for ulcer relief.

Remember to pay careful attention to the unique aspects of your project plan. And, do not forget that there is a direct relationship between the product requirements—i.e., the PBS—and the work content of the project.

> Thinking about the scope of the project at hand, Sam recalled the effort required for getting a clear statement of the project objectives. It was necessary to build a raft to carry the family, all the household items, fifty sheepskins of grain, thirty sheep, twenty geese, ten goats, five asses, two oxen, and one aged mother-in-law.
>
> But there were other questions to be asked. What would be the size of the flock—and the family, for that matter—by the time the raft will be completed? Must all of these items be transported at once, or could they be transported in several trips? If it had to be one trip, what would be the size of these critters by the time the raft was completed? Could the animals be tethered, or would they have to be contained within the structure? And on and on.
>
> Finally, Sam decided to make a product breakdown structure of physical features and functions. Then a sketch of the raft could be made on a slab of stone. With these in hand, if the size of the flock or the family changes, appropriate recognition could be sought in a rational manner.
>
> ### Product Breakdown Structure of Physical Features and Functions
>
> **Security**: Raft must be large enough to carry enough members of the family across on one trip to establish security of its new site and build a corral for the animals.

Safety: Raft must be large enough to provide safe passage for family and animals.

Environmental Friendliness: Minimize the number of trees cut.

Performance: The *ilities*

☐ **Usability**: Must be easy to steer with only one crew member aboard.

☐ **Availability**: Must be available on a continuous basis for a period of one month.

☐ **Repairability**: Any repairs must be able to be done by the one crew member.

☐ **Maintainability**: Should require no maintenance during planned usage period, but inspections should be feasible daily to ensure integrity.

Power: Should use the flow of the river to maneuver the raft back and forth across the river.

Using these requirements, Sam then developed a conceptual sketch of the raft to share with the other members of the project team. This would give them all an initial vision of what they were going to build. It would provide a basis for discussing the pros and cons of this version. In this discussion, they could develop alternatives that might be more effective, as well as efficient, to produce. (Many years later, this process would be given names such as "project team alignment" and "value engineering.")

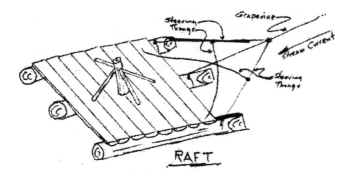

Sam also prepared a preliminary bill of materials to aid the team in understanding the implications of the design concept. One thing that became clear in this process was that the concept design was too small. It would take sixteen medium logs instead of just four.

Preliminary Bill of Material for Raft

3 large logs, 3 hands across, 15 paces long (main beams)

16 medium logs, 2 hands across, 12 paces long, split in half (floor boards)

1 short log, 2 hands across, 2 paces long (post)

4 small logs, 1 hand across, 2 paces long (post supports)

48 hide strips, 3 fingers across, 3 paces long (fasten floorboards to main beams)

8 hide strips, 2 fingers across, 3 paces long (fasten supports to floorboards)

1 hide strip, 2 fingers across, 8 paces long (fasten supports to post)

2 hide strips, 3 fingers across, 6 paces long (steering controls)

3 hide strips, 6 fingers across, 10 paces long (towing bridle)

1 grapevine (can be several pcs), 800 paces long, strong enough to hold five people hanging from it (tow line)

Sam heard that a WBS could help define the work to be accomplished, but sought a better way to describe the product of the project. Sam would still have to learn how to develop this document.

APPENDIX VII.A—
MARS PATHFINDER PROJECT

MISSION OBJECTIVE AND PROJECT REQUIREMENTS

2.1   The MESUR Pathfinder Mission Objectives

The Pathfinder mission objectives are derived from the need to validate both technical and managerial approaches that would ultimately be applied to follow-on landers. The Pathfinder objectives fall into three categories: 1) engineering, 2) scientific and technology, and 3) managerial.

2.1.1   Pathfinder Engineering Objectives

   a. Demonstrate the cruise, entry, descent, and landing system approach that would be applied to safely place a lander on the Martian surface.

2.1.2   Pathfinder Scientific and Technology Objectives

   a. Characterize the Martian surface morphology and geology at meter scale.
   b. Obtain information of the elemental composition of rocks.
   c. Obtain information on the structure of the Martian atmosphere from measurements of pressure, temperature, and acceleration during entry and descent. Obtain surface meteorology information by operating the temperature and pressure sensors after landing.
   d. Deploy and operate a microrover flight experiment to evaluate the effect of the Martian surface conditions on the rover design and the rover's ability to deploy and operate scientific instruments.

2.1.3   Pathfinder Management Objectives

   a. Complete the development phase of the project within the total cost of $171M ($150M FY '92S) exclusive of microrover development costs.

b. Establish the management approaches, processes, and procedures needed to develop a system in a quick-reaction, fixed-price, low-cost mode that can be carried forward as the development mode for follow-on landers and future Discover missions.

2.2 Project Requirements

In satisfying the general engineering, scientific, and management objectives of Section 2.1, Jet Propulsion Laboratory (JPL) shall implement the MESUR Pathfinder Project, within the budgetary and schedule constraints described in Section 2.3.2, to meet the following specific requirements:

a. Launch a single flight system to Mars during the 1996 opportunity.

b. Acquire engineering data during entry and return of this data after landing.

c. Acquire atmospheric structure data (pressure, temperature, and acceleration) during entry and descent and return of this data after landing.

d. Return engineering data on the condition and configuration of the lander after landing.

e. Operate the lander and return science and engineering data for a minimum of one month with a goal of one year on the Mars surface, including:

   1. Acquisition and return of a 360-degree panoramic image of the Martian surface.

   2. Demonstration of the operation of the Code C-funded microrover on the Martian surface for a minimum of one week with a goal of one month. Includes taking an image of the lander to aid in assessing the landed condition, deployment and operation of science instruments, and collection of data to assess rover performance on the Martian terrain.

3. Deployment and operation of the science instruments required to meet the science objectives stated in Section 2.1.

2.3   Project Constraints

In satisfying the mission objectives and the project requirements, JPL shall meet the following constraints.

2.3.1   Mission Design Constraints

The primary mission design and navigation constraints for the MESUR Pathfinder mission, and those accruing to Pathfinder through a requirement to demonstrate key systems and technologies for Network, include:

a. The injection energy requirements and dimensions of Pathfinder vehicle shall not exceed the capabilities of the Delta II (7925) launch vehicle.

b. The transfer trajectory at injection shall contain a bias to reduce the probability of the accidental impact of the launch vehicle upper stage with Mars consistent with the adopted planetary projection requirements.

2.3.2   Budgetary Constraints

The MESUR Pathfinder Project shall be conducted within the following budgetary constraints:

2.3.2.1   Development Phase

a. Total: NASA shall provide JPL with a development phase budget of $171 million for the design and development of the MESUR Pathfinder Mission. The development phase budget begins with new-start approval and extends through thirty days after launch. ... several services and items are not included within these costs.

b. Fiscal year: Funding available to the MESUR Pathfinder Project by fiscal year (real-year dollars) shall be as follows:
   1. FY '94: $58.5M
   2. FY '95: $76.3M
   3. FY '96: $35.9M

2.3.2.2 Mission Operations and Data Analysis Phase
a. Total: NASA shall provide JPL with a mission operations and data analysis (MO&DA) phase budget of $14 million (real-year dollars) for the operation of the MESUR Pathfinder Mission. The MO&DA phase budget begins at launch plus thirty days and extends to Mars landing plus one year. As described in Section 3.3, several services and items are not included within these costs.
b. The funding profile for the MO&DA phase is determined by a mission that launches in a twenty-day window starting in December 1996 and lands on Mars in July 1997, employing a Type 1 trajectory. The resultant MO&DA phase cost profile by fiscal year is as follows:
1. FY '97: $8M
2. FY '98: $6M

2.3.3   Schedule Constraints
Level 1 control milestones are listed below:
a. Project Start   October 1993
b. Complete Project Critical Design Review   July 1994
    (serves as Launch-2 year review)
c. Complete System Text Readiness Review   July 1995
    (serves as Launch-1 year review)
d. Ship Pathfinder to KSC   October 1996
e. Launch Window   December 1996/January 1997
f. Complete Thirty-Day Mission   August 1997
g. End of Project   August 1998

2.3.4   Product Assurance Constraints
To achieve the project objectives within the cost and schedule constraints, the flight system will be designed and built to JPL Class C product assurance requirements. The instruments and the microrover will be designed and built to JPL Class D requirements. JPL and NASA acknowledge the additional risk associated with these classes, the limited redundancy, and the entry, descent, and landing events.

2.3.5   National Environmental Policy Constraints
The MESUR Pathfinder Project shall not use radioisotope thermoelectric generators, but may use radioisotope heating units as heat control devices. The use of such nuclear material will be limited to an amount consistent with preparation of an "environmental assessment report" versus an environmental impact statement.

2.3.6   Metrication
All MESUR Pathfinder Project elements shall use SI units during the design, fabrication, test, launch, and operations of the Pathfinder mission. Exceptions to this policy can be granted by waiver if implementation of the policy is cost prohibitive, such as in the use of existing equipment and design.

APPENDIX VII.B—
MARS PATHFINDER PROJECT

PROJECT SCOPE MANAGEMENT

The Mars Pathfinder project concept was to build a spacecraft that would demonstrate the cruise and entry, descent, and landing approach to be applied to safely place a lander, equipped with a science investigation payload, on the surface of Mars. Once on the surface, the main objectives were to transmit a single partial panoramic image and successfully deploy and operate a robotic rover with autonomous navigation capability.

The project scope was centered upon achieving the mission success criteria, which were established and assigned weights, based on the importance of each criterion to the Office of Space Science at NASA. The criteria were as follows:

❑ successful landing and return of entry, descent, and landing engineering telemetry (70 percent)
❑ acquisition and transmission of a single, partial panoramic image (10 percent)
❑ successful rover deployment and operation (10 percent)
❑ completion of a 30 sol (Martian day) primary lander mission; completion of all additional engineering, science, and technology objectives (10 percent).

In addition, the Advanced Concepts and Technology Office at NASA had the following specific mission-success criteria for the rover team:

❑ Complete a 7 sol primary rover mission on the surface.
❑ Take at least one successful alpha-proton x-ray spectrometer measurement of a Martian rock and a Martian soil sample.

The project scope was based on a capability-driven design instead of a requirements-driven design. The mission, flight, and ground system designs were strongly driven by existing hardware and system capabilities in order to achieve cost and schedule restraints. The Pathfinder implementation also included the use of concurrent engineering, where the development of flight hardware and software, MOS hardware and software, and test hardware and software proceeded in parallel, rather than in the traditional series arrangement.

Chapter VIII

The Work Breakdown Structure

Sam received a message that a schedule and cost estimate is required for the project before proceeding with execution. Suddenly it became clear that building a raft was serious business that had to be carefully managed. Not enjoying doing a lot of work for others without adequate recognition (especially for an in-law), Sam proceeded to document the project.

First, the functions to be performed by the raft were listed on a piece of birch bark using a burnt stick. Realizing that the cost of building the raft increased faster than the increase in its size, Sam decided to make it small, even if it requires multiple trips across the river. Therefore, a means of returning it to the landing on this side of the river was needed. Second, the sketch of the raft was elaborated by detailing the parts that were required to make the completed raft. From these drawings, a bill-of-materials was developed.

With this basic information in hand, Sam was ready to develop a work breakdown structure (WBS).

PREPARING TO DEVELOP THE WORK BREAKDOWN STRUCTURE

Projects today are often quite large and complex. Failure to plan the project carefully can result in excessive rework and interminable delays in completion. Failure to communicate the plan can lead to confusion and uncoordinated efforts. Failure to define what is a part of the project, as well as what is not, may result in work being performed that was unnecessary to create the product of the project, and thus lead to both schedule and budget overruns.

A Vision

Today, the project manager is expected to develop a clear vision of the product of the project *and* of the project by which it will be created. This is an important notion.

The vision of the product of the project may be static in nature—what it will look like when it is completed. This can be represented in a three-dimensional physical model or as a graphic version from that on a computer screen. Soon it will be possible to create such an image via holography.

The vision of the project is dynamic in nature, incorporating successive views of the product as it takes shape, first conceptually, then as drawings in two and three dimensions, and finally as a three-dimensional graphic of the progressive steps in producing that product. This final representation can be driven by a project network diagram-based schedule. (For a discussion of one of the earliest applications of this concept, see the showcase project article, Project Management at the Minnesota Department of Transportation, *Project Management Journal*, 1988.)

A sketch of the product clarifies what is desired. (See an interview with Jeana Yeager in the showcase project article, Voyager, by Swanton, *Project Management Journal*, 1988, for a description of the significance of a sketch drawn on a napkin.)

For many products, a bill-of-materials (BOM) may be useful in understanding the sketch in more detail. It can be a simple, unstructured *materials takeoff* or *engineering BOM*—i.e., just a simple list of parts that must be assembled. Alternatively, it may be useful to prepare a simplified *manufacturing BOM* that, through its structure, illustrates how you plan to assemble the pieces of the product. This can be developed in a top-down or bottom-up manner, or a combination of the two.

The listing and analysis of the functions to be performed provide a clear statement of what the product of the project is to perform. In purchasing, this is known as specifying the performance requirements. The United States (U.S.) Army Rock Island Arsenal has described a more formal approach, known as the functional flow-down diagram. For a software project, a structured programming diagram may serve the same purpose. For a movie, a general storyboard, identifying the setting and actors, may be most useful. Each technology has its own set of tools that helps depict the product of the project. During this process, many decisions are made that will be critical in managing the project.

THE WORK BREAKDOWN STRUCTURE

> Work Breakdown Structure (WBS): a product-oriented "family tree" of project components that organizes and defines the total scope of the project. Each descending level represents an increasingly detailed definition of a project component. Project components may be products or services (PMI Standards Committee 1996).

Lists must be one of the oldest of management tools. While birch bark may have been the medium of choice at one time, the backs of envelopes soon took over that role. Only recently has the process been formalized, in part because of the desire to develop better management tools based on it. Thus, the WBS was invented, defined, refined—and perhaps defiled.

The primary purpose of the WBS is to aid the project manager in managing the project. Its concept is as simple as the answer to the question,

141

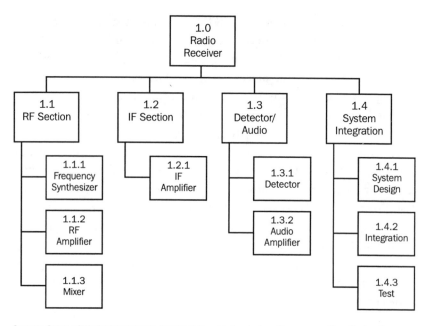

Source: Scope of Work Management, Sandia National Laboratories, Albuquerque, New Mexico, Oct. 1991, p. 10.

FIGURE VIII.1

An Example of a Work Breakdown Structure

"How do you eat an elephant?" Answer: "One bite at a time!" The WBS is a tool for dividing the elephant into bite-sized pieces. It looks similar to a family tree, with each generation being called a level. The top level is usually designated *level 0*, the next one down *level 1*, and so on.

It is easy to confuse the WBS with two similar documents: an organization chart and the structured BOM. While they may appear similar, there are important distinctions:

❑ A WBS portrays the deliverables except at the lowest level of any branch where the work packages portray the work to be done. It likely contains items that are necessary for the project but will not appear in the product of the project per se, such as inspection and test reports.

❑ The organization chart portrays the relationships among people who may be responsible for performing the work of a project. An element in an organization chart may be responsible for one or more of the elements in a WBS.
❑ The structured BOM portrays only the objects that will be produced as the work is done and will actually be in the product.
Three different functions—three different tools.

Developing the Work Breakdown Structure

The mechanical aspects of developing a WBS are quite simple. Napkins or the backs of envelopes are still useful devices. Additional discipline is added by introducing a hierarchical concept, permitting attention to be focused on different levels of detail as the process proceeds. A word processor provides a flexible tool with automatic indentation (via tabs) but with the convenience of easy change and adding extra space where required. A more sophisticated approach involves the use of project planning, scheduling, and control software with a built-in capability for developing and displaying the WBS in either an indented list or a family-tree format. This software has the advantage of interfacing directly with a project network diagramming capability. However done, by focusing primarily on one higher-level element at a time, the ability to think about the lower-level elements required and avoid omissions is greatly enhanced.

A schematic of a WBS is shown in Figure VIII.2.

The Purposes of the Work Breakdown Structure

A project consists of the sum total of all of the elements of the WBS. Conversely, an element that is not contained in the WBS is not a part of the project. Any work that cannot be identified in the WBS requires authorization to proceed, either as a recognized omission or as an approved change-order.

The WBS is, first and foremost, a tool to be used by the project manager to manage the project. While there are differences of opinion on this issue, it is the OC's opinion (one we have confirmed with several other

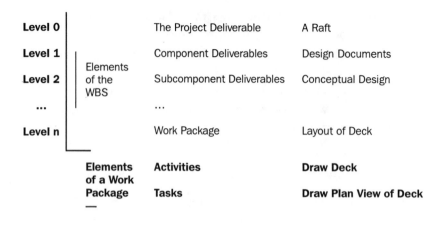

FIGURE VIII.2
Schematic of a Work Breakdown Structure

practitioners) that *the WBS should not be used as a financial accounting tool, per se.*

Some writers suggest using standard WBSs across all projects to permit the collection of costs in such a manner that they can be compared across projects. This is the position of the U.S. Department of Defense—at least to some degree. Our opinion is that this unnecessarily constrains the project manager in performing the project in an optimum manner. There are other methods that can be used to collect costs for comparison across projects and financial accounting purposes. *The accounting on the WBS should be aimed solely to aid the project manager in applying earned value measures of planned versus actual costs.*

There are several ways by which either financial accounting or comparative analyses of deliverables can be achieved. One of these is in the coding of work packages or activities. If the same code is used to identify a type of work, similar activities can then be compared across projects with even more meaning than comparing level 1 or 2 WBS elements. This also provides a more meaningful way to develop an estimating database. Another alternative is for accounting to map WBS elements to its own, shall we suggest, financial breakdown structure (FBS) or component breakdown structure (CBS). The FBS or CBS might not need to go below level 3 to collect these costs.

Similarly, some organizations perform large numbers of projects, all of which are similar. To reduce the time required for planning a project, a master WBS is used. This is a reasonable practice if the project manager is allowed to adapt the master to recognize specific differences between projects and in the assigned resources. The best approach would be to allow the project manager to propose those changes desired and, if the changes are adequately supported, be allowed to adopt them. The act of defending the need for change leads to a higher level of commitment to make it work.

Accordingly, the WBS must focus on the work to be accomplished to complete the project. At each level, the WBS elements should normally be specific deliverables. Level "0" is the end product of the project. Level "1" may be components of the end product, but may also be a document that portrays the results, conclusions, or recommendations of a phase of the project. This is consistent with the U.S. Department of Defense's Defense Systems Acquisition Review Council procedure, the practice for managing the development of new pharmaceuticals, and in the stage-gate procedure for new product development. Also, certain costs, such as project management, that cannot be directly related to lower-level WBS items can be collected in WBS elements that do not deliver a product per se.

Sequential relationships between elements, work packages, or activities are not shown in the WBS. Such temporal or technological relationships are shown in the project network diagram. The manner in which the WBS is structured can have major impact on the way that the project is executed. First, consider some rules that must be followed when developing a WBS.

RULES FOR DEVELOPING A WORK BREAKDOWN STRUCTURE

The usefulness of the WBS is directly dependent upon its ability to communicate accurately. Reports prepared based on the WBS must accurately represent the facts as to progress, status, and potential future progress. To do this, there must be some standard for the preparation of a WBS to ensure that it means the same thing to all the people using it. The following rules will assist in achieving the required accuracy.

Uniqueness: An element of work is associated with one and only one higher-level element. Care must be exercised in this regard to avoid duplication of work or budget.

Summative: The work content of an element is the sum of the work content of all its immediately subordinate elements.

Unity of responsibility: Each element should be the clear responsibility of a single individual. Use specific names and titles. Where the identification of the specific performer is unclear, especially in a matrixed project, the identification of the next higher-level individual should be used. One of the most effective and timely efforts by a purchasing function observed on a project identified the vice president of purchasing as the responsible person. He was determined to not be guilty of holding up the project.

Motivation by involvement: It is well established that involvement in planning leads to motivation to perform to the plan. That does not mean that every project participant has to be involved in every stage of planning. A level-by-level process with participants, including those responsible for two levels higher in the WBS, should provide adequate communication and feedback upward if problems are identified.

Documentation: The WBS is a communications device. Precision and assurance of communication are greatest when reduced to writing. It should be approached in much the same manner as writing a contract with an outside agency, without all the boilerplate. A part of this documentation must be the coding structure of the WBS, so all project participants can—indeed, should be required to—refer to the appropriate WBS element in all work and work products. (See Scope Management Through a WBS: Key to Success for the Logan Expansion Project, *PM Network*, 1993. This project was selected as the Project Management Institute 1994 Project of the Year.)

Consistency of definitions: To ensure ease and accuracy of communications, the definition of terms should be consistent over the entire WBS and, ideally, across all projects performed in an organization.

Utility of the WBS: Above all, the WBS must be useful to all who will refer to it in performing the project, from responsible supervisory personnel to the highest level of management that will oversee the project and, of course, to the client. Branches need go only to the level of detail necessary for effective management of the work. Indeed, the WBS can be considerably more detailed on immediate work and summary on future work, adding detail as understanding of future work becomes clearer.

Baseline control: Finally, for this discussion, all essential stakeholders should approve the WBS as the definitive statement of both the necessary and sufficient work content of the project. This then provides the baseline against which the inevitable changes to scope are approved and documented.

THE PROJECT TEAM

By this time, you should know the nature of your project charter and who will be the key people on the project team. Knowledge of these people's specific skills and talents can have an impact on exactly how you develop the WBS and how you choose to organize your project. Similarly, consider where your project falls on the continuum from projectized to weak matrix. For example, if it is totally projectized, you will likely have more flexibility in assigning responsibilities. In a matrix organization, you may have less control over which individuals work on some aspects of your project, and so you should conform work-package definitions to the organizational elements that will actually perform the work.

The number of people working on your project will also have an impact, as smaller projects can be managed with somewhat more flexibility than larger projects.

Sometimes the project charter will dictate the composition of the team. On the other hand, you may have the opportunity to select the individuals for your team. The capabilities of the people on your team may influence exactly how the work is organized and thus effect the way that you define the WBS. The optimum plan should take advantage of the strengths and weaknesses of the individuals to the greatest extent possible. Often, tradeoffs will have to be made, due to the availability of key individuals as they rotate off of other projects.

Many projects are composed of the efforts of several subcontractors and vendors. Care should be taken to match the WBS to the unique capabilities of these suppliers. For example, it is often desirable, where possible, for all components of major items to be supplied through a turnkey contract. This can substantially reduce the hassles and finger pointing involved when the item does not perform as required. Contractor capabilities and availability become especially important when the work has to be performed in less-populated geographic areas, or when the number of possible contractors is small. For example, on a major casting plant, delays were encountered because there was a single supplier of a major component and much of its capacity was absorbed by a contract that was placed a few months before the contract on the subject casting plant was let. An excellent example of effective recognition of contractor capability and availability was documented in the showcase article, The Endicott Oil Field, *PM Network*, December 1987.

PROJECT STRATEGY AND THE WORK BREAKDOWN STRUCTURE

The WBS is a means for the project manager to define the strategy by which the project will be performed. Some of the strategy is dictated by technology. For example, a school building's structural system was largely precast concrete. One beam weighed some 120 tons. It was precast in the basement and lifted three stories by two large cranes. This dictated the sequence of much other work to provide access for the cranes until that beam was in place. On a software project, it may be important to design, code, and test many utility routines prior to completing coding on most application routines. In preparing a Ph.D.

dissertation, it may be important to keep all chapters moving ahead concurrently, lest developments in one chapter require a rewrite of another chapter.

Some strategic decisions are a result of the resources that can be brought to the project. Some are a reflection of the political pressures, real and potential, internal and external, that the project faces. Some are personal preferences of the project manager. The personal preferences should be based more on the project manager's weaknesses than strengths, a consideration that grows in importance with the magnitude of the project. While the project manager is likely selected due to specific strengths, designing the project strategy based on the project manager performing lower-level responsibilities can result in an unbalanced view of and inadequate attention to other problems and opportunities that are inherent in any project.

The project manager must be concerned with determining the direction of the project, the methodologies for decision-making and the degree of personal involvement, and recognizing and solving problems before their impact on the project becomes significant. The WBS provides a major opportunity to deal with these concerns.

A Metaphor for a Work Breakdown Structure

It is convenient to think of a WBS as a stack of billiard balls. Imagine using a billiard ball rack and thirty-five balls. Stack them to make a three-sided pyramid. The balls represent the elements of the WBS. The work inside the ball is well suited to assignment to a specific individual. The project manager should be primarily concerned with the work at level 1 of the WBS. Similarly, the person responsible at the level above guides the work in each successively lower level in the WBS. At each level, some attention should be given to lower levels to ensure that accurate communication has taken place.

The points of contact between the balls represent the direct interfaces between the elements. These occur at the same level and at successive levels. Points of contact between levels are where direction and guidance are required by the responsible person at the level above— the formal lines of responsibility. Conflicts and misunderstandings of this type tend to surface rather naturally, although the wise project manager assumes that they will not and takes action to cause them to surface.

The points of contact between balls at the same level, and especially between balls that do not touch a common higher-level ball, are where there are likely to be the most misunderstandings, conflicts, and delays in the project if not tended properly. An example of such a misunderstanding, and its impact on the project, involves the design and development of two interacting printed circuit boards. One was under the direction of a computer scientist and the other, an electrical engineer. It was agreed that a set of 256 values was needed for the required functionality. The computer scientist, based on the usual practices of computer design, defined the domain as being from zero to 255. The electrical engineer defined the domain to be from one to 256. This difference was sufficient to prohibit the effective interfacing of these two elements. The impact on the project was about $600,000 worth of rework. Once again, we have a vivid example of the alternative way to spell *assume*.

One criterion of a good WBS is that the points of contact between balls at the same level (think of this in hyperspace) should be minimal. The more such points of contact, the more time the project manager will have to spend providing coordination between elements in the WBS.

The interstices between the balls represent the undiscovered or unassigned work to be done. Even the most routine project has such interstices, largely due to the unique nature of projects. As the size, complexity, innovative technology, urgency, and other characteristics that contribute to the uniqueness of the project increase, the greater the likelihood, magnitude, and difficulty in identifying the content of these interstices. Although the project manager must be primarily concerned with the interstices at the next level down, some attention should be paid to such interstices at every level of the WBS. This will identify any undiscovered work content of the project while it is still just smoke—before it becomes a full-fledged fire.

All of these aspects of projects require considerable attention by the project manager, first to minimize the potential problems, and, second, to identify them early in their development. The project manager must design the planning, scheduling, and control system in such a way as to force recognition of problems of this type before they cause damage to the project. Managing-by-walking-around is one of the most effective ways to ferret out these potential problems. The most effective approach to minimizing these problems is to design the WBS in a manner that minimizes their potential. This is the essence of strategic planning of a project.

SELECTING THE PREFERRED WORK BREAKDOWN STRUCTURE

The project manager should prepare more than one alternative WBS down to the third level. Analyze and document the pros and cons of each, considering the above discussion. Performing this analysis explicitly in this disciplined manner will minimize the natural tendency to rely on a successful past experience or personal prejudice, and ensure an adequate consideration of the unique characteristics of the project at hand. An exception to this would be where a project is very similar to a past project. In such a case, the previous WBS might be used. However, it is advisable to review the analysis that was performed on the previous project to ensure that the same criteria prevail in the new project and that the judgments made then are still applicable.

A FINAL THOUGHT

While the WBS is an essential element to provide stability of a project, it must be recognized that projects are used to manage change. Change in the project is usually inevitable, as learning happens during the life of the project. Consideration should be given in developing the WBS for how changed requirements and work content will be incorporated into the approved WBS. Change control is essential. The anomaly of projects is that, while they are the means for instituting change, change itself creates many of the problems on projects.

Using the product breakdown structure of physical features and functions, sketch, and bill of materials, Sam listed the objectives and other considerations that would be important in deciding how to manage the building of a raft. Then three WBSs were developed down to level 3.

1. Safe Approach	2. Fast and Efficient	3. Compromise
Raft	Raft	Raft
Model	Design	Design
Build	Concept	Concept
Test	Detail	Detail
Deck	Gather materials	Gather Materials
Materials	Logs	Logs
Prepare materials	Hides	Hides
Assemble	Grapevines	Grapevines
Movement	Prepare materials	Construct
Rope	Logs	Fabricate
Thongs	Hides	Assemble
Blocks	Grapevines	Movement
Test	Assemble	Prepare Materials
Float	Deck	Assemble
Movement	Movement	Test
	Test	
	Float	
	Movement	

Each WBS was evaluated on a three-point scale: good, bad, and indifferent. Based on this analysis, even though it required more work by Sam, the fast and efficient approach was chosen.

EVALUATION OF ALTERNATIVE WORK BREAKDOWN STRUCTURES

CRITERIA	EVALUATION		
	1	2	3
Project Duration	B	G	I
Cost	B	G	I
Conformance to Specs	G	B	I
Risk/Design	G	I	I
Production	B	G	I
Conflict	G	B	I
Resource Utilization			
Human	G	B	I
Materials	G	B	I
Specialization of Skills	B	G	I
Commitment	G	G	I
Design Effort	G	B	I
Coordination/Integration by PM	G	B	I

APPENDIX VIII.A—
MARS PATHFINDER PROJECT

WBS	WBS Title	WBS	WBS Title
10000	Project Management	50000	Assembly Test & Launch Operations
11000	Management & Administration	5AD00	Plans & Procedures
13000	Planning, Assessment, & Integration	5AG00	GSE and Facilities
18000	Education & Public Outreach	5AK00	KSC Operations
99000	Project Reserves	5AM10	Engineering and Management
20000	Project Engineering	5AM90	Reserves
21000	Management & PET	5AP00	Pasadena Operations
22000	Mission Design & Navigation	70000	Ground Data System
23000	Mission Engineering	71000	Management
24000	EEIS Engineering	72000	System Engineering/Administration
25000	Configuration Management	75000	Loan Pool (H/W & Licenses)
30000	Flight System	79000	Reserves
39000	Flight System Reserves	7H000	Hardware
3A000	Attitude & Info Management	7W000	Software
3AH00	AIM Hardware	7X000	Operations Support
3AW00	AIM Flight Software	80000	Mission Operations System
3AX00	AIM Subsystem Engineering	81000	Management
3C000	Telecommunication	82000	Requirements & Design
3E000	Product Assurance & Safety	89100	Reserves
3F000	Management & Engineering	8E000	Experiment Team MO Spec. Develop
3L000	Entry, Descent, & Landing	8N000	Engineering Team MO Spec. Develop
3M000	Mechanical Integration S/S	8T000	MOS Test Training & Operations
3P000	Power & Pyro Switching	M0000	Mission Operations & Data Analysis
3R000	Propulsion	M1000	Management
40000	Science & Instruments	M9000	Reserves
41000	Management	ME000	Experiment Team Operations
42000	System Engineering	MG000	GDS Maintenance
43000	Science Teams	MM000	MOSO Support
49000	Reserves	MN000	Engineering Team Operations
4A000	Atmos Structure & MET	MX000	Science Data Analysis
4L000	Lander Imager	R0000	Rover System
4X000	APX Spectrometer Instrument	R1000	Management
4Y000	APX Deployment	R2000	System Engineering
		R4000	System Integration & Test
		R7000	Mission Ops & Data Analysis
		RC000	Control & Nav Subsystem
		RM000	Mechanical Subsystem
		RP000	Power Subsystem
		RT000	Telecom Subsystem

FIGURE VIII.A
MESUR Pathfinder WBS to Level 4

Chapter IX

Planning—
The Project Network
Diagram Approach

Plans are nothing; planning is everything.

Dwight David Eisenhower

Sam now had an understanding of what had to be done. There was a work breakdown structure (WBS) of the major items that had to be delivered. He wondered, "How long will it take to do all this?"

It was now time to develop a road map. Sam had done some simple projects previously on which there was only one resource: Sam. To figure how long these projects would take required simply adding the times to perform each activity, one at a time. For this project, it would require 1,998 days. Sam realized that this would be unsatisfactory, as the project would hardly be completed before the next snow fell.

Sam was again feeling uncomfortable.

Sam thought of the day that a bunch of chariots came by and what had happened when they did not have a road map. They came back to ask where to go. It had been a traumatic experience to see such a formidable force become confused. When the leader was asked to explain the objectives of the group and the road map to get there, the only answer received was "huh?" Sam knew this armada was in trouble. After lengthy questioning, Sam finally determined where the group wanted to go and suggested a way to get there. Sam told them to "ride hard" and bade them, "Good journey!" Little did they know that Sam had given them a plan whereby they were sure to go off the deep end, for Sam said very quietly as they rode off in the dark, "Go jump in the lake!"

The moral of the story, to Sam, was: "If you don't know where you want to go and how you want to get there, any damn fool can give you directions to show the world that you are all wet."

INTRODUCTION

Any given project can be accomplished in a number of ways. One observation on this proposition is: "There's the government's way, the right way, and my way." The wise team member will recognize this statement as the declared "end of discussion." However, that does not mean that the project will in fact be done "my way." Indeed, one of the values of planning is gaining agreement of all participants on how the project will be done. Without this agreement, there will be a variety of perceptions regarding how it is going to be done, leading to low efficiency or even chaos. *A good plan that is less than the best, but well understood and agreed to by those who are going to perform it, will likely produce better results than the best plan that lacks understanding and agreement.*

The earliest of planners must surely have been among the most intelligent of the day with special capabilities to integrate the many activities of a project over time. Even today such people have significant advantages in discussions of project timing. The epitome of such an individual was a gentleman who was responsible for scheduling die production for new model cars at Chrysler in the sixties. His unique ability to see the relationship between activities and equipment across many plants—both in-house and supplier—enabled him to provide quick (and generally relatively accurate) answers to scheduling questions. More accurate answers can be obtained, by less-gifted individuals, from network-based techniques.

Again, one of the anomalies of projects is that while they are the means of creating change, change in the project is the most likely cause of problems and poor results. Yet, change is an inevitable fact of life on projects of any significant magnitude. We learn while performing the project; we learn from other projects. Laws, regulations, and societal expectations change during the project. Technologies and other knowledge advance while the project is being performed, creating a risk that the product of the project will be obsolete before the project is completed. Thus, it is essential to incorporate changes into the project whenever appropriate. This places a premium on a technique that can facilitate changes to our plans. Network-based planning techniques provide that capability.

As projects became larger in magnitude and complexity, even the most adroit schedulers had difficulty processing the myriad of details involved. A new language of planning was required. In the early fifties, a new language—project network diagramming—was developed that proved quite successful in a variety of applications. Using this language, the resulting plan can be described as the *road map* for the project. Among its many advantages are the ability to analyze alternative schedules and even alternative plans, reduce total project duration, reduce costs, and gain greater assurance that the project can be completed as scheduled.

The computer was an integral part of these systems, as they all required substantial computational capability. Thus, the computer was at once a significant contributor to and a serious constraint on the development and use of this new language of project planning and control. Primitive computers, as well as primitive systems employing project network diagramming hindered many early applications of project network diagramming. Developments in both computers and project management software have overcome most of the problems of the past.

It is essential that project personnel and executives of modern organizations have skills in using this new language of project planning and control. They must be skilled in planning, scheduling, asking penetrating questions, analyzing, rescheduling, and taking appropriate actions to manage the projects, given new tools that are more precise and sensitive.

THE BASIC CONCEPTS OF PROJECT NETWORK DIAGRAMS

Appendix IX.A—Some Historical Perspective, presents a review of the development of networking techniques. The reader may wish to review this material before proceeding, as it explains some terms in this section that may not be familiar.

Early in the OC's experience with modern project management (MPM), he explained the concept—on a Friday—to a person, George, in the training section of the Corporate Personnel Office. On Monday, George related the following:

I always like to test new ideas on my wife. She had been an officer in service and I was an enlisted man. I explained project management to her on Friday evening, and I think she got the idea. Saturday morning, I found a piece of paper at my breakfast place with a diagram on it that looked like this:

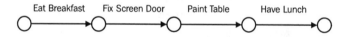

She explained the diagram to me, saying, "We are going to have breakfast. After we finish breakfast, you are going to fix the screen door. After you fix the screen door, you are going to paint the table. After you paint the table, we will have lunch. If you don't fix the screen door and paint the table, there ain't gonna be no lunch."

I think I explained it to her too well!

While the diagram may not have been necessary to get this simple message across, it certainly was vivid. Such diagrams can be even more useful in communicating the work that must be done to complete a larger project. A similar project with a bit more complexity shows what Sam might have had to do to prepare lunch.

For Sam, fixing lunch was perhaps a larger project. It might have been diagrammed as shown.

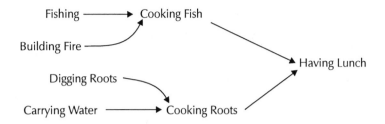

A *project network diagram* (PND) is a schematic display of the sequential and logical relationship of the activities that comprise a project. Generally, these relationships should be due to technological considerations that are very difficult to violate.

For example, if getting oneself dressed in the morning is considered a project, it just does not make sense to put your shoes on before your socks. It is generally a matter of preference whether to put on both socks and then both shoes, or to complete the left foot before the right foot. Putting both socks on at the same time and then both shoes at the same time is feasible, provided additional resources are used. In MPM, a network diagram is used to portray these technological sequences and permit consideration of alternative schedules and/or plans. Figure IX.1 shows the use of networks to describe alternative ways of putting on socks (RSock and LSock) and shoes (RShoe and LShoe).

Example C, in Figure IX.1, does not imply that both socks are put on simultaneously, although that is certainly a possibility. Rather, it provides the flexibility to determine the actual sequence based on other criteria. It is important for planners to focus on technological relationships to prevent implicitly scheduling a project before really understanding the available alternatives. Note that the project duration implied by this PND could only be achieved with additional resources. Example D would be nonsensical in most instances, for it implies not only putting the sock on the left shoe, but also putting both socks on the left shoe.

This rather trivial example illustrates one of the basic notions of networks: parallelism or concurrency. Much of our prior experience with projects has been with serial projects—i.e., working on only one

A. RSock ⟶ LSock ⟶ RShoe ⟶ LShoe ⟶ Done ⟶

    Serial network with preference for putting both socks on first and doing the right foot before the left foot.

B. RSock ⟶ RShoe ⟶ LSock ⟶ LShoe ⟶ Done ⟶

    Serial network with preference for putting sock and shoe on right foot first.

C. RSock ⟶ RShoe
                 ↘
                 Done
                 ↗
LSock ⟶ LShoe

    Parallel network with only technological relationships.

D. RShoe ⟶ LShoe ⟶ LSock ⟶ LSock

    A nonsensical network, in most instances.

FIGURE IX.1

Examples of Network Diagrams

activity at a time and finishing it before starting the next one. Generally this has been due to the use of only one resource: ourselves.

Often we have recognized that there were alternative ways in which the project could have been performed, but we generally viewed them as alternative plans rather than alternative schedules for the same plan. For example, look at C in Figure IX.1; the time required for putting on both socks and shoes could be reduced by having two persons doing these tasks. Indeed, this presents the opportunity to consider the larger project of getting dressed, for the dressee could be performing some other task, such as tying a tie or placing a kerchief in a pocket, while the socks and shoes are being donned.

There has been much confusion about project network diagrams. It will be helpful to clarify these issues before proceeding. Because they are a result of several historical events, it may be helpful to review the historical developments that lead to the confusion before proceeding further. They are discussed in Appendix IX.A at the end of this chapter.

The Essential Conventions

The three distinct areas of ambiguity that emerged as a result of differences in these techniques are:

1. The graphic language for portraying the plan.
2. The identification notation.
3. The focus of the techniques and their computations performed on the plan—i.e., on the events or the work content.

The techniques will be discussed in a later chapter after a discussion of the basic computations. The conventions are best understood by the three-dimensional diagram shown in Figure IX.2.

The *graphic conventions* are activity-on-arrow (AOA) and activity-on-node (AON). AOA is illustrated in the networks in Figure IX.1, Figure IX.3 and Appendix Figures IX.A.1, 2, and 3. AON is illustrated in Figure IX.4 and Figure IX.A.4 and is the preferred convention in this book. Note that an activity requiring no time or resources in AON is synonymous with an event in AOA. Thus, it is easy to establish checkpoints, milestones, major milestones, and the like in AON.

The *focus* can be on the events or on the work. Figure IX.A.1 is strictly event oriented. Figures IX.A.2, 3, and 4 are work oriented. (Further discussion of these techniques in *PM 102* will make this clearer.)

With AOA, the *identification convention* can be on the "i" (or "j"), if the focus is on the events. If the focus is on the work (or activities), it can be identified by pairs of "i"s and "j"s—i.e., the end points of the activities represented by arrows. With either AOA or AON, the activities can be identified by a name assigned to the activity without reference to the bounding events. Figure IX.A.1, 2, and 3 are "i-j" oriented, if the event numbers are used as the means of identification. Figures IX.A.2 (if the letters are used to identify the activities), 3, and 4 are focused on the activities.

Tabular Listings

To perform the basic calculations on these activities, and for other purposes, it is convenient to put the activities in a list format. This is illustrated for the examples in Appendix IX.A, as well as in the examples here.

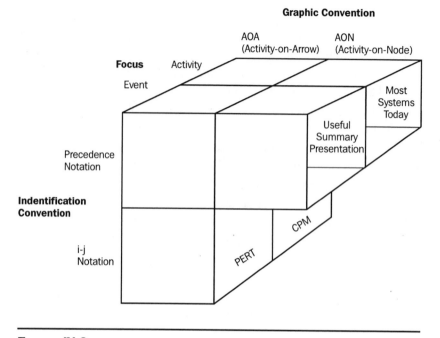

FIGURE IX.2
The Essential Conventions

Early software had some strenuous requirements in coding including that all "i-j" identifiers had to be numeric, and the "i" of an activity had to be less than the "j" of that activity. This sometimes caused serious problems when a major replanning of a project was required. That is not a problem today. Current systems permit the use of alphanumeric codes to uniquely identify activities; thus, an activity can be given the code name "ABCDE," or "AESS." The relationship between two or more activities can be specified by simply listing the activity of concern followed by its predecessor(s), such as:

AESS – ABCDE, 34567, CM12P

In the past, some knowledgeable persons argued for a nonmeaningful code that led to the likes of "ABCDE." More recently, it has become an accepted practice to use a meaningful code such as "AESS," which might stand for "Erect structural steel in Area A." Recently developed software provides several characters for identifying activities, making it quite easy to develop a standardized coding structure for activities commonly performed in an organization. This provides at least two benefits: ease of recalling the names of frequently used activities, and the ability to compare like activities across projects to improve estimating and performance measurement.

Note that in early PNDs it was required that there be only one starting event and one completion event in a project. Today there can be many starting activities and many ending activities.

Clearly, precision in communicating can be gained by referring to these three conventions, which clearly define the alternative networking concepts. For example, from this point on, all examples will be portrayed using AON, focusing on the work and identifying the activities. This has been a conscious decision for several reasons:

❑ Planning time: Experience indicates that an AON network can be developed in as little as one-fifth of the time it would take for the comparable plan in AOA.

❑ Accuracy: An experiment, albeit rather unsophisticated, led a planning analyst, who was a very strong advocate of AOA, to convert to AON after graphing several logic exercises in both modes. Not only did he complete the AON versions much more quickly than the AOA versions, but also the AON versions were more accurately portrayed than were the AOA versions.

❑ Changes: Changes can be incorporated more easily. If activities must be subdivided, the relationship of the more detailed activities to the original activity can be maintained.

❑ Familiarity: The AON concept is more common to most people, as it is comparable to industrial engineering flowcharts and computer-program logic diagrams.

❑ Better schedules: Planning can be separated from scheduling more effectively, thus better utilizing the capabilities of project management software to develop a better schedule based on a plan that is better, since the plan is less influenced by possibly fallacious assumptions about the schedule requirements.

❑ Less training required: All of the above leads to less training time required in AON to achieve a given level of competency in network development.

❑ Overlaps easier: Overlaps are easier to use in AON mode. (They are discussed in the next section.)

❑ Compatible software now: When project management software on microcomputers was introduced, most of them were in AON mode. AON has now become the de facto standard.

Before leaving this subject it should be made clear that the AOA network has some very useful characteristics; for example:

After planning a project using AON, it is very useful to check the logic of the plan by obtaining a computer-generated plot of the project plan in AOA mode on a time scale to see the temporal relationships between activities. Often it is possible to recognize that an activity is plotted at what seems to be a totally illogical time. This can easily happen in a complex project, because a precedence relation was inadvertently not specified, or one was specified that was really not necessary.

Top executives, in planning corporate strategy and approving projects, are primarily concerned with: "When is it going to be completed?"—i.e., events. Generally, they have too many other details on their minds to consider much more than the major milestones of the various projects ongoing in the organization. Indeed, there has been an axiom that no more than three milestones on a project should be reported on at a briefing of top executives, lest they become confused from information overload. However, recent interest in *prudence*, especially in utility rate cases, has led top executives to take more interest in the major projects in their organizations. The OC expects that, as MPM is used more in the executive suite, there will be a growing interest in somewhat more detail.

Thus, AOA is important to understand and will be referred to later where its use is most advantageous.

Overlap

In addition to the above conventions, some alternative logical relationships are available. The original planning logic permitted only one basic logic between activities: the follower of an activity cannot start until the preceding activity is finished. This proved quite frustrating in accurately portraying relationships where the follower could clearly start before the predecessor was finished. Thus, four alternative logics were introduced and are popular today. They are shown as activities with their predecessors.

Finish-to-start with overlap/delay—[B A (FS – 3 days)]—activity "B" can be started three days before activity "A" is finished, or for [B A (FS + 3 days)], activity "B" cannot start until three days after "A" is finished. The former is useful to indicate that detail drawings can be started three days before the layout drawings are completed. The latter would be convenient for indicating that the forms cannot be removed from a concrete wall until three days after it was poured. This eliminates the need for the activity *cure*.

Finish-to-finish with overlap/delay—[B A (FF + 3)]—is convenient to indicate that it is all right to start activity "B" before "A" is finished; just do not expect to finish it until three days after "B" is finished.

Start-to-start with overlap/delay—[B A (SS + 3)]—is an alternative way to state that work can start on detail drawings three days after layout drawings have started.

Start-to-finish with overlap/delay—[B A (SF + 3)]—might be used when the first work on activity A is checking the feasibility of some design element before releasing the work product of activity B.

While these overlap capabilities are very useful in many situations, they can be overused. A network incorporating many of these relationships can be very confusing and thus diminish its ability to communicate. Manual calculations are much more involved, thus reducing the ability to analyze the network. Finally, it is easy to incorporate logic that has unintended consequences. Indeed, in the extreme, it has been shown that it is possible to construct a network that has a finish time before the start time. With these thoughts in mind, it should be easy to remember to use these relationships with discretion.

PLANNING WITH PROJECT NETWORK DIAGRAMS

Experience has demonstrated an interesting phenomena when teaching the use of project network diagrams (PNDs). The example does make a difference. If it is a construction example, software people believe that it does not apply to them. If it is a pharmaceutical example, movie people believe that it does not apply to them. And so on. Thus, we have selected a, perhaps nonsensical, project with which anyone can relate. It illustrates the basic concepts of PNDs and some of the calculations that can be performed on them. Consider a simple project that involves collecting some data while driving from New York to Los Angeles in the United States (U.S.). Theoretically this trip of 2,846 miles can be done in 43 hours and 45 minutes. This was determined using the Rand-McNally software package *TripMaker* (1997). This assumes that the trip could be driven nonstop at the following speeds: interstates at 65 miles per hour (mph), U.S. highways at 55 mph, and state highways at 45 mph. Clearly, this is not really feasible without some very special arrangements and a very high level of dedication on the part of the people involved.

Suppose we split this trip into three segments with intermediate stops at Chicago, Illinois, and Cheyenne, Wyoming. The choice of Chicago and Cheyenne as intermediate points is based on an intuitive guess (looking at a map) that the three legs are approximately equal in length, and it is feasible to drive them in one long day each. The distances in miles are 796, 965 and 1,103 (differences in total distances are due to the legs being to city centers). The driving times are 12:28 (hours: minutes); 15:07; and 17:12. The differences are not as large if after Chicago the driving speed is increased by 10 miles per hour, resulting in a driving time of 13:02 and 14:47 for the second and third legs. Regardless, these are long hours for driving. They could lead to fatigue, inaccurate data collection, and perhaps to an accident.

This is an excellent example of a linear project with only one activity in process at a time. Very simply, we can visualize this project as three activities: 1) driving from New York City to Chicago, 2) from Chicago to Cheyenne, and 3) from Cheyenne to Los Angeles, California. It is easier to think of these segments individually than to think of the entire trip at one time. It is also easier to set the appropriate parameters more precisely, such as driving speed. Nevertheless, these three segments form a linear set. The first segment must be finished before the second segment can be started, and the second segment must be finished before the third segment can be started. Because this is a linear project, simple travel programs such as *TripMaker* can calculate the total time required for completing this project.

In the previous section, we discussed project network diagramming (PND) with the example of putting on shoes and socks. How could this driving project be portrayed in a PND? The simple trip could be described in AOA notation as three activities, as shown in Figure IX.3. The three segments or activities could be described, focusing on the start and completion of each activity, in "i-j" notation as 1–2, 2–3, and 3–4. Alternatively, they can be identified, focusing on the work to be done, as New York to Chicago, Chicago to Cheyenne, and Cheyenne to Los Angeles.

These segments can be portrayed and identified more simply, as shown in Figure IX.4, as A, B, and C or, mnemonically, NYCh, ChCy, and CyLA.

Clearly, considering additional detail would allow a more even distribution of the work content by any measure. Depending upon our expected use of the diagram, it might be better to identify this project in smaller segments. An extreme of this is shown in Table IX.1. (This detail was generated by *TripMaker.*) This level of detail would be quite useful in actually driving from New York City to Los Angeles. It would be useful in executing any project, especially when scheduling specific resources. There is so much detail, however, that it really is not very useful in general planning.

The PND in Figure IX.5 is more useful at this stage, because it captures the essence of the plan without a lot of confusing detail.

The activities in this PND could be more precisely defined as:

- NYCl   driving from New York City to Cleveland
- ClTo   driving from Cleveland to Toledo
- ToCh   driving from Toledo to Chicago
- ChDM   driving from Chicago to Des Moines
- DMOm driving from Des Moines to Omaha

□ OmCy driving from Omaha to Cheyenne
□ CySL driving from Cheyenne to Salt Lake City
□ SLLV driving from Salt Lake City to Las Vegas
□ LVLA driving from Las Vegas to Los Angeles.

The logic of the PND can be defined by showing the followers of each activity as:

Activity	Follower
NYCl	ClTo
ClTo	ToCh
ToCh	ChDM
ChDM	DMOm
DMOm	OmCy
OmCy	CyLV
CySL	SLLV
SLLV	LVLA
LVLA	—

The first line in this listing can be interpreted as "when NYCl is completed, ClTo can begin." The absence of a follower of activity LVLA indicates that it is an ending activity in the project.

The PND can also be defined by showing the predecessors of each activity as:

Activity	Predecessor
NYCl	—
ClTo	NYCl
ToCh	ClTo
ChDM	ToCh
DMOm	ChDM
OmCy	DMOm
CySL	OmCy
SLLV	CySL
LVLA	SLLV

These lines can be interpreted as "driving to ClTo cannot start until after NYCl driving is completed." In this case, the absence of a predecessor to activity NYCl indicates that it is a beginning activity of the project. Both of these conventions are useful. *The OC generally prefers the predecessor notation based on the proposition that it is more rea-*

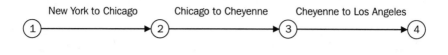

FIGURE IX.3

The Activity-on-Arrow Project Network Diagram

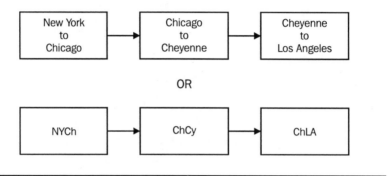

FIGURE IX.4

The Activity-on-Node Project Network Diagram

sonable to hold a person responsible for knowing what must precede her activity than knowing what can be done after her activity is completed.

Now consider a redefinition of the project. Suppose our objective is to count the number of a certain type of billboard within a hundred-mile radius of each of the nine cities on the route. This might make it possible to complete the project sooner, if we are willing to incur some additional costs and use more resources. Specifically, suppose we use three people, flying one to Chicago and one to Cheyenne, where each rents a car and proceeds on their segments. It would cost more, but the project could be completed earlier. To ensure quality, we could have a one-hour training session in New York City before leaving. Then all three could get in the same car, stopping at the Newark Airport, where the two air travelers would separate and the first driver would continue. This introduces parallelism into the project, as all three could proceed on their segments independently. The PND for this plan would thus appear as illustrated in

Road	Direction	Miles	Time	Distance
Start in New York, NY				
BROADWAY/8TH AVE	SW	1	7:02 AM	1
ST495/LINCOLN TUNNEL	W	3	7:06 AM	4
ST3 to I-80	N	12	7:18 AM	16
I-80	W	58	8:13 AM	74
I-80/DE WTR GAP BRDG	W	1	8:14 AM	75
I-80 to OHIO TPK	W	333	1:28 PM	408
I-80/OHIO TPK	W	76	2:37 PM	484
I-80/I-90/OHIO TPK	W	142	4:48 PM	626
I-80/I-90/INDIANA TOLL RD	W	79	6:01 PM	705
I-80/I-90/INDIANA TOLL RD	W	56	7:51 AM	761
I-80/I-94	W	19	8:10 AM	780
I-80/I-94/KINGERY EXPWY	W	1	8:11 AM	781
I-80/I-294/TRI-STATE TLWY	W	5	8:16 AM	786
I-80	W	143	10:29 AM	929
I-280/I-74	W	9	10:37 AM	938
I-74	W	3	10:40 AM	941
I-74/IA-IL MEM BRDG	W	1	10:42 AM	942
I-74	W	5	10:47 AM	947
I-80	W	161	1:21 PM	1108
I-235	S	14	1:35 PM	1122
I-80	W	120	3:28 PM	1242
I-80/I-29	N	3	3:31 PM	1245
I-80	W	156	6:01 PM	1401
I-80	W	716	5:57 PM	2117
I-80	W	38	7:35 AM	2155
US40/US189	E	18	7:52 AM	2173
US189	S	29	8:22 AM	2202
I-15	S	599	5:42 PM	2801
I-10/SN BER'DINO FRWY	W	43	6:24 PM	2844
US101/HOLLYWOOD FRWY to				
Los Angeles,CA	N	2	6:26 PM	2846

Parameters Used:
Speeds (mph): Interstates, 65; U.S. Highways, 55; State Roads, 45
Hours: Start 7:00 AM; Finish 6:00 PM + or – 60 minutes

TABLE IX.1

A Detailed Plan for Driving from New York to Los Angeles

Figure IX.6 (using only the original three segments). Now we have three
people away from home, so it is necessary to fly them back before the
project is completed.

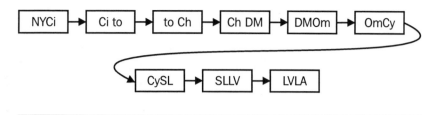

FIGURE IX.5
A More Detailed Project Network Diagram

Note that in this example, there has been no explicit consideration of the time required to perform these activities, or to setting target or required completion times. This allows us to think only about the logical relationships between the activities. Furthermore, in general, there is no single duration for performing a given activity. For example, while the actual driving time might be constant, the total elapsed time required to drive from Newark to Chicago may vary, depending upon the number of hours we drive per day and the speed we drive, both controllable variables. In addition, it may vary depending upon the weather, traffic conditions, car problems, and a host of other variables. The latter are all relatively uncontrollable variables leading to uncertainty in the duration. There is even a relationship between the controllable and uncontrollable variables in that if we get behind schedule due to an uncontrollable variable, we are likely to drive more intensely in an effort to make up time.

Another way to further improve performance on the project is to add additional resources. Suppose we have a branch office in Pittsburgh, Pennsylvania, and can call upon more people there to join in the project. They could leave downtown Pittsburgh together in one car and drive to the airport. Two could be dropped off to fly to Chicago and Cheyenne. A third one could be driven north on I-79 to the intersection of I-80 and join the person who was driving from Newark. The driver would then return to Pittsburgh. These three would not receive training, but they would each be working with a person who was trained.

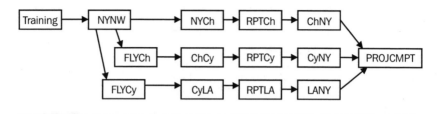

FIGURE IX.6

A More Complex Project

These changes in the project would add to the complexity of the network, as shown in Figure IX.7. Note that we have split activity NWCh into two parts—NWCh1 and NWCh2—to recognize the pickup at the intersection of I-80 and I-79, and added the activities PiAPT and APT80, to get the persons to the airport and up to I-80, and 80Pi, to get the car and driver back to Pittsburgh. Thus, we have included the work content and costs involved. PiAPT, FLYCYa, and FLYCha get the two people to Cheyenne and Chicago, APT80 gets one person to I-80, and 80Pi returns the car and driver to Pittsburgh. Thus, we have identified all the work, resources, and costs.

Note that this plan results in two starting activities for the project. The activities without predecessors are recognized as start activities and are automatically assigned the project start time for scheduling calculations. Similarly, activity PROJCMPT is unnecessary and could be eliminated. The activities without followers would be recognized as ending activities and are assigned project target completion dates. In calculations, all these activities must be completed for the project to be completed. Thus, the latest such activity determines the earliest that the project can be completed.

This project plan raises the question, "When should the people from Pittsburgh leave the office?" Perhaps we want to brief them at the conclusion of the training in New York City. This could be shown as an arrow from "Traing" to "PiAPT." If their departure can be delayed, perhaps they can get some work done at the office before leaving. Or perhaps they have a meeting they have to attend before leaving. This could be noted by posting an earliest start date on "PiAPT," representing

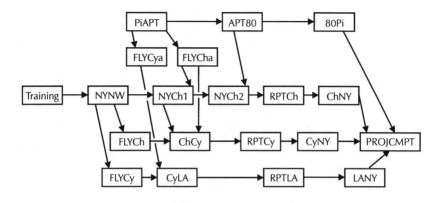

FIGURE IX.7
An Even More Complex Project

when the meeting is expected to end, or by a preceding activity representing the meeting. Another constraint on this is when the person driving from Newark Airport will arrive at the intersection of I-80 and I-79. On the other hand, if we do not want him to delay the project, he may have to leave earlier than the people leave New York, due to flight schedules. In addition to how long it takes to fly from Pittsburgh to Chicago or Cheyenne, we must consider when the planes depart Pittsburgh that will arrive in Chicago and Cheyenne without otherwise delaying the project. These questions can be dealt with in modern project planning and scheduling software.

We have used a simple mnemonic method of identifying activities such as NYCh to represent the activity of driving from New York City to Chicago. This is advantageous, as it requires the writing or reading of only four characters as opposed to as many as twenty-nine characters (thirty-three, counting spaces) required for the description. Furthermore, we were able to distinguish between flying from Newark to Chicago and from Pittsburgh Airport to Chicago by simply adding a suffix: "a." While this may be trivial in this example, in a realistic project it can be significant. With a little ingenuity, it is feasible to develop a coding structure that makes it easy to identify tasks quickly and easily on a given project.

Most organizations perform a rather limited number of operations. In this example, there were only four: 1) training, 2) flying, 3) driving, and 4) reporting. These could be identified simply as T, F, D, and R; operations performed at a specific sight and on a specific object. Sites can be identified geographically by map location or by coordinates. In the example, we have used cities to identify sites. On a construction project, a matrix can be superimposed over the total site and the HVAC system divided by cell in the matrix. In developing a computer program, the total system can be divided into separate subsystems, and so on. Thus, an operation is performed on a site and/or an object. Because each project has a limited number of operations, sites, or objects, it is relatively easy for the participants to learn a simple coding system that permits them to communicate precisely and with relatively little effort. Consider the time required for writing the few characters necessary to identify a specific activity versus writing the description of that activity. It should be a conscious and deliberate decision regarding how activities are going to be identified on a particular project. Note that some experts have argued against such a coding structure.

Some Other Conventions

Orientation on the page. When viewing the above PNDs, they conflict with our perception of a road map. New York City is the easternmost point on this trip; yet it is shown to the left, which is normally west on a map. The convention is that projects start at the left side of the page and end on the right side. In general, move from the upper-left corner to the lower-right corner. Sometimes it is desirable to start nearer to the vertical center of the page, placing activities above and below to minimize the extent to which logic arrows cross. In the early stages of developing a PND, do not worry too much about this. Get the logic on paper, and clean it up later. Just avoid excessive sloppiness.

Arrowheads. All arrows must have arrowheads. Otherwise, direction of the constraint will be unclear from the diagram.

Documentation. Do take the time to completely identify all papers used in developing the network diagram. There will be occasions when questions will arise as to why the project plan is defined in a specific way. The working papers will be useful. If that question comes up in court, they will be essential.

With this mundane example, we have introduced the basic concepts of the PND. It can be as simple as we want it or as complex as our intended usage of it requires. Note that the more we are concerned with the usage of resources, the more detail that is required. (The calculation of possible scheduling alternatives will be discussed in *PM 102*. First, we need to consider some planning misconceptions and identify some good practices.)

PROJECT PLANNING MISCONCEPTIONS

Planning and Scheduling Are One

Probably the most serious misconception of project planning is that it includes scheduling; planning and scheduling are two distinctly separate processes. If combined, much of the value of using modern tools will be lost. Many key decision-makers in business and government have no appreciation for this fact and blithely set intermediate target dates for parts of the project, believing they are practicing good management. They believe they are *motivating* the project team. Seldom do they have any knowledge of the impact that these targets will have on the success of the project.

It was with considerable disappointment that the OC heard a representative of an outstanding research institute describe how he liked to plan a project. His approach was, using a chalkboard, to establish a time scale along the bottom, indicate major milestone dates, and then start plotting each activity according to the amount of time that he felt was available for it. Having completed that step, he would put the results in a critical path method (CPM) system. He might as well have not bothered. Neither the plan nor the schedule was reliable, as they were largely based on wishful thinking—wishing that the activities could be done in the allotted time.

Planning Is Done at the Top

The old view of management is that only those at the top of the organization are capable of planning. Not only is this passé, but it is counterproductive. First, it assumes that the sole source of knowledge is at the top. While it may be true that it takes both breadth and depth of knowledge and experience to get to the top, much of that knowledge and experience is obsolete by the time of the executive's *arrival* at the top. It often is based on "that's the way we did it back when I was pushing a broom." It likely is not the way it should be done today. Second, it assumes that those below don't know or care. If this is indeed the case, it is both a very bad reflection on the quality of managing that has been performed by those at the top and a leading indicator of an organization headed for failure.

Planning must include participation of doers; they probably know better ways of getting the job done. With the exception of a very few, lower-level employees really do care about the project, both out of pride and economic self-interest. And, there is nothing like involvement in planning to create motivation to perform to plan.

Long Lead-Time Items

Many have the attitude that if they take care of the long lead-time items, the rest of the project will take care of itself. The folly of this is well stated in the legend concerning the lack of a nail for the horse's shoe.

While it is true that early attention to long lead items is important, it is also equally true that great auto races are often lost because of the failure of a ten-cent part. Besides, committing too early on the long lead items may freeze the project into a less than desirable project strategy. It took some adroit planning to change from structural steel to prestressed concrete construction on the Pontiac Silverdome stadium—and still meet the original cost and schedule.

Probably the most important aspect of long lead items is reserving critical resource capacities as early as possible to avoid them being overcommitted at the time they are required. A major casting plant project was delayed as a result of a competitor gaining commitment of the critical resource about a month before the casting plant project had progressed to the point of committing on the same items.

Plans Are Cast in Concrete

Prior to CPM, the standard technique for managing projects was a manually drawn Gantt chart. On a project of significant magnitude, this would consist of a master schedule with perhaps fifty bars on it. It was not unusual for each of those bars to be supported by another sheet of fifty bars. It is easy to imagine the labor hours required to reschedule such a project; thus, they were seldom rescheduled. This no doubt led to the reputation of Gantt charts "concealing more than they revealed." As the project plan changed gradually over time, mental notes were made of the net impact on the schedule "as published." Only if reports that the project was on schedule became absolutely incredible, or if there was a major scope change, would the project be replanned and scheduled. Thus, for all practical purposes, it was cast in concrete.

Today, a CPM-type program permits the user to establish a baseline (essentially cast in concrete) plan and schedule, but then permits changes to the operational plan and schedule that provide an accurate picture of how the project is being, and likely will be, performed. Published schedules can be realistic, and reports of progress can be accurately interpreted. At any time, the current plan can be compared to the baseline plan to determine the difference from the original commitments.

GOOD PRACTICES

How Should the Project Be Performed?

This is probably the most important guide to effective project management and yet one of the most difficult to get people to actually do. Two examples of successes as a result of following this dictum are almost ancient history now.

The first example was a major project at Chrysler's Defense Engineering. The chief engineer directed the top twelve people on the project team, working in a large conference room, to develop a project network diagram that described the best way to execute the project. It took them two weeks of intense effort. By the time they had finished, they agreed that, "for the first time, all the key people on the project team knew how they were going to do the project." Project execution then proceeded without a hitch.

The second example was the construction of the Pontiac Silverdome, an approximately $50 million effort utilizing an as-yet-untried roof concept, fabric panels buoyed up by a positive air pressure inside the dome. Shortly after groundbreaking, the operating engineers went on strike. The project manager was told, "Never mind the strike, you build this thing on paper as many times as you can to get the best project plan you can." He went to the construction trailer daily and did just that. As a result, that project—a fixed-price, fast-track job—was completed on schedule and within budget in spite of a major design change. After some of the foundation work had been completed, the design was changed from structural steel to a precast, prestressed, and poured-in-place concrete structure. The road map was solid, and the changes were incorporated quickly.

To develop the best plan for a project requires a clear understanding of the objectives of the project. Generally, project objectives are defined in terms of time (duration), technical performance, and cost. In a later chapter, we will examine this in more detail. For our purposes here, just consider these three and assume that technical performance is the primary objective.

Develop the Plan as It Ought to Be Done

In general, for any activity, there is an optimal duration for its performance. Trying to reduce this duration results in greater costs. Taking longer to perform it also increases costs. In addition, the higher the desired technical performance, the greater this optimal duration. Thus, given the technical objectives for an activity, there is an optimal duration. All activities should be estimated based on this standard.

Similarly, for any pair of related activities, there is an optimal sequence in which they should be done. This should be based only on technological requirements, i.e., conceptual design must precede detail design, forms and rebar must be in place before concrete can be poured, and so on. It is tempting to include other constraints in the network at this time such as resources—e.g., *a priori* sequencing two activities requiring the same resource. This sequencing is better left to the resource analysis process while scheduling the project. Likewise, constraints of the "it would be nice to" variety should be avoided at this stage.

Let the Scheduling Software Help You Make the Tradeoffs

Ideally, the objective of planning in this case should be to understand what is the best way to achieve the technical performance objectives of the project if there were no serious constraints on time or cost. Having this understanding, it is now possible to revise the plan to meet the other project objectives. For example, a major administrative computer-based system project required the transmittal of a large number of documents for review and approval. Activities were included in the network for intracompany mail, each estimated at three days; fifty of those ended up on the critical path. It was an easy decision to change from intracompany mail to hand delivery. (While that might be achieved by fax or on computer today, the phenomenon is still relevant.) If project completion is more important than total cost, additional or more proficient resources might be assigned to critical activities. On the other hand, if cost is the critical variable on the project, the least expensive approach should be sought.

Clearly, such tradeoffs should be made deliberately with full consciousness of the impact on the other variables of the project. This is very evident when considering another project variable: risk. Often, the best plans include many activities for inspecting, checking, testing, and so forth. Sometimes it may be acceptable to eliminate some of these activities. Inherently that means an increase in risk. It may be possible to use an alternative approach to protect against that risk. For example, it may be a policy for all drawings to be checked by a single individual. That responsibility could be shifted to a management person (covered by overhead costs instead of direct labor costs), but two things need to be recognized: the checking is not likely to be as thorough, and the time required will detract from other managerial responsibilities.

Thus, trying to combine scheduling with planning will inevitably obscure many decisions about cost, technical performance, and risk, as well as incorporate much wishful thinking that the schedule is in fact feasible.

KISS Principle

The keep-it-simple, stupid (KISS) principle is still an important admonition. That does not mean that less is always better. It does mean not to make it any more detailed or complicated than is necessary for the purpose intended. It also implies creating a project network diagram for each level of the project WBS or of management, if the two are not reasonably equivalent. (More on that later.)

Plan Only to the Level of Detail Necessary

A way of managing the degree of detail required is to think in terms of the report recipients. For example, consider a major, in-house project.

The board of directors meets once a quarter. Members are primarily interested in what has been accomplished and that appropriate progress will be achieved in the interim until their next meeting—i.e., milestones. It is probably appropriate to report to them on three to five major milestones per meeting. At least one of those should have been achieved since the last report, and at least one should be starting before the next meeting. Thus, the network at that level should have sufficient detail to meet their needs.

The CEO should be kept informed at least one level below that on a monthly basis—i.e., three to five milestones per month. A most useful admonition is to ensure that your CEO is not *surprised* by a question from a board member. This rule can be extended to any level of the organization and to the client.

Members of the project executive committee, probably a subset of the organization's executive committee, should be provided with reports a level below the CEO's, plus the operating-level detail of those activities for which their area is responsible. Thus, we now have need for three levels of detail: 1) the board, 2) the CEO, and 3) the project executive committee members. These events should be built into the project network from the beginning. On most projects, it should be possible to report against these events for the entirety of the project. It is below this level that most changes will occur. (This discussion will continue in *PM 102* under reporting methods in project control.)

The next level could be called the operational level. The project manager should get weekly reports at this level. Generally, it should be one level above that at which detailed resource assignments and allocations are made and scheduled. If that additional level of detail, which we will call the tactical level, is required by the project manager, it is readily available; however, the primary users of that level would be those professional employees, and the supervisors of the nonprofessional employees, who actually perform the work.

Modern project planning and scheduling software facilitates creating reports of these types with relatively little effort if the WBS and the project network diagram are properly developed in the beginning.

Planning by the Work Breakdown Structure Level

The above discussion provides one rationale for the level-by-level WBS approach to project network diagram development. Another rationale is the discipline it provides. One person, after spending a couple of days drawing a network starting from the beginning of the project, asked, "How do you get the thing to come back to an ending?" Without the level-by-level discipline, she kept incorporating detail at lower and lower levels, causing the network to explode. As soon as she focused on one level of the WBS, she was able to maintain a consistent degree of detail and quickly moved to the ending of the project.

Planning By the Work Breakdown Structure Work Package

A useful technique for developing a project plan is to plan each WBS work package separately and then integrate them into a single large PND. A work package is "a deliverable at the lowest level of the work breakdown structure. A work package may be divided into activities" (*PMBOK® Guide*). The advantage is that the planner can focus on that one work package, giving greater assurance that all necessary activities will be included. The downside is that, in the process of integrating, some constraints that span work packages may be overlooked. It is helpful to include in the work package PND the recognition of predecessors that must be completed before your activity can start. For example, doing detail drawings may require that the layout drawing be completed. Alternatively, it may only be necessary that specific aspects of the layout be completed. These can be identified graphically and notationally as interface events. They must be connected to the preceding activity in the interfacing process.

Planning by the Rolling Wave

Not all activities need to be defined at the same level of detail at the beginning of the project. Initial emphasis should be on the detail necessary to get the project started and on long lead-time items. As the project is further defined, the future details can be added with greater accuracy. Nevertheless, care should be exercised to plan the entire project at a sufficient level of detail to provide reasonable accuracy in estimating the total costs of the project to ensure a proper baseline plan.

The Project Planning Process

There are four basic directions in which the project can be planned: 1) forward, 2) backward, 3) top down, and 4) bottom up. All of these have merits and should be used in combination for best results.

Top down may be quick, but it often ignores the intelligence and experience of people lower in the organization. It is important to use it to some degree to ensure that overall project strategic decisions are incorporated in the plan.

Bottom up permits broad input by all working on the project. People at lower levels will tend to develop conservative approaches—i.e., longer durations and more checking activities. This will be exacerbated if the organizational climate is one that severely penalizes failure to perform to schedule. Also, the project manager needs to be involved in the process to ensure that appropriate strategic issues are considered.

Forward planning is starting at the beginning of the project and planning how to get to its completion. While this is certainly appropriate, there will be times when it may be more expeditious to use **backward planning**. In this, you start at the completion of the project, or a phase, and focus on what must be accomplished to achieve that objective or to permit an activity to start. In general, people know more about what work must be completed before they can proceed on their activity than they know about what work can proceed once their activity is completed.

It is wise to use more than one of the above-mentioned techniques—such as both forward and backward planning—to minimize the omission of work or constraints, as well as the inclusion of unnecessary work or constraints.

There are two types of activities to which the project manager will want to give especial attention: high-risk and high-visibility activities. Both can cause real headaches in the execution of the project, and attention to them at the early planning stage can minimize later headaches.

High-visibility activities include things such as high-level meetings or activities for which there may be considerable public attention. An example of the latter was the stringing of the cables supporting the roof of the Pontiac Silverdome stadium. These cables were strung with the aid of a helicopter, and many local citizens drove close to the site to watch. There were also television news cameras present during the day. Any missteps would have been embarrassing at the least, especially if someone were hurt.

Projects often include major meetings with high-level executives, politicians, and the like. These meetings are often preceded by a number of activities merging just before the meeting. The more activities merging, the greater the probability that at least one of them will be late, thus either delaying the meeting or conducting it with less than everything completed. One planner in the styling division at Chrysler always inserted an activity between the merging activities and major meetings. He called such an activity "water." It was simply the recognition that something was going to be late and to provide some time to allow for it—sort of a contingency allowance of time. Today there are more sophisticated ways with which to deal with this phenomenon, but it should not be forgotten.

SUMMARY

The PND approach to planning projects is one of the most significant elements of MPM. It improves communications and is flexible and computer compatible. On the one hand, it is very simple. On the other hand, there is much to learn to realize its many benefits in practical application. A PND can become very complex, not because of the PND language, but because the projects we undertake are complex. Furthermore, we add complexity as we try to perform projects in less and less time. However, without the capabilities of modern project planning and scheduling software, we would be severely challenged to accomplish many of today's projects in the time and with costs that we do and achieve the technological results we have learned to expect.

Given the importance of planning to modern societal efforts, it is important that these approaches to planning be well understood by all involved in managing projects. Project managers must be particularly adept at developing and analyzing PNDs. The project manager should not be expected to develop the plan in all its detail. The project manager should always review the entire PND, paying particular attention to those portions that are unique, entail significant risk, and have high visibility.

Sam struggled with this network-planning concept and after several tries came up with a PND for the raft project. Since it was drawn in the dirt on the floor of a cave, it was subject to change if new information became available. It was definitely a feasible plan.

RAFT

Design
    Concept   DC
    Detail design   DDD
Gather Materials
    Logs   GML
    Hides   GMH
    Vines   GMV
Prepare Materials
    Logs   MPL
    Hides   MPH
    Vines   MPV
Assemble
    Deck   AD
    Movement   AM
Test
    Deck   TD
    Movement   TM
    Final Test   TFT

APPENDIX IX.A—
SOME HISTORICAL PERSPECTIVE

In the early fifties, there was considerable discussion of how to improve the performance of projects. There were a few academicians who were discussing theoretical approaches including the use of connected graphs, a branch of mathematics. Other academics were looking at traditional industrial engineering techniques of flow-charting. Some practitioners had gained experience using the line-of-balance technique. Some practitioners were simply seeking new tools to understand projects and their scheduling. While these efforts were largely uncoordinated, they resulted in at least five different development efforts.

The most publicized effort was under the auspices of the U.S. Naval Weapons Systems Laboratory at Dahlgren, Virginia. They developed a technique called program evaluation and review technique (PERT) for application on the Polaris Missile Weapons System (Malcolm, et al. 1959). PERT was developed to better understand the status of the Polaris Missile Weapons System Program. As its name implies, its primary purpose was to analyze existing plans to determine the probability that the plans would be executed per schedule. It involved three time estimates to assess the uncertainties associated with the duration of each activity and thus the probability that a significant event would be accomplished per schedule. It was *event oriented*, as there was less concern about what the work content was than with when it was likely to be completed. It used a graphical network language similar to *activity-on-arrow*; however, the activity and its work content was of less concern than the time required to get from one event to another. Each event was given a numerical identity. A pair of these numbers, "i-j," was used to identify the logical relationships between events represented by the arrows—i.e., the activities. A simple PERT PND is shown in Figure IX.A.1. Activity 20–30 is a dummy activity, requiring no time nor resources but necessary to portray accurately the logical relationship among these activities.

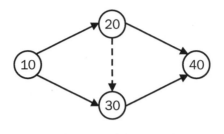

FIGURE IX.A.1
A Simple PERT Project Network Diagram

A concurrent effort at DuPont, with assistance from UNIVAC, led to the development of a critical path planning and scheduling system (CPPS) that received considerable publicity, although less than PERT (Kelley and Walker 1989). CPPS was developed to better plan and manage the construction of new and maintenance of existing chemical plants. It truly used activity-on-arrow graphical notation and "i-j" identification notation but was work oriented; i.e., it focused on what work had to be accomplished to get from "i" to "j." The work is denoted by activities named A, B, C, and D, as shown in Figure IX.A.2. It did not focus on probabilities but rather on the time-cost tradeoffs (see *PM 102*) for individual activities that would allow the project to be completed sooner with the least increase in cost. While significant improvements in project performance were reported, the efforts required to estimate two times and two costs (to define the time-cost tradeoff curve) for each activity precluded widespread use and led to the simplification of just one time estimate. Practitioners knew this modification as CPM, while academicians knew the original time-cost technique as CPM.

Another effort by the Air Force Ballistic Missile Command and Wright-Patterson Air Force Base resulted in a system called PEP. It was similar to CPM except for the network diagramming technique. Each real activity was uniquely identified by its own "i" and "j," while the relationships between activities was portrayed by dummy activities. (Dummy activities are typically shown as dashed lines, while real activities are solid lines.) Thus, the total number of activities, real and

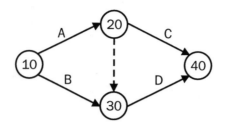

FIGURE IX.A.2

A Simple PERT Critical Path Planning and Scheduling System/Critical Path Method Project Network Diagram

dummy, necessary to portray a given plan was much greater in PEP than it was in PERT or CPM, as seen in Table IX.A.1.

Meanwhile, independently, Professor John Fondahl at Stanford University and Professor Bernard Roy in France were developing comparable capabilities using precedence networks. The effort at Stanford was aimed at developing a better way to describe and schedule construction projects. This effort relied on the more common *flowchart* used in industrial engineering and general systems analysis. The graphical notation became known as activity-on-node diagramming, and the identification notation focused on the activity rather than on its end points. The calculations involved were the same as in CPM.

It is common practice to consider the left side of an activity as representing its start, and the right side as representing its completion. Note the similarity between a PEP PND and an AON PND. In Figures IX.A.1, 2, and 3, a real activity is shown as a solid arrow bounded by "i," representing its start, and "j," representing its completion. Logical relationships (i.e., not involving any work) are shown by dummy activities. In Figure IX.A.4, a box shows an activity with its start on the left and its finish on the right. Logical relationships are shown in Figure IX.A.3 by arrows having the same characteristics as the dummy activities.

Due to the publicity and training in PERT provided by the U.S. Department of Defense, AMA, and others, this became the popular

Figure 1 & 2	Figure 3	Figures 2, 3, & 4 (predecessor notation)	(follower notation)
10-20	1-10 (dummy)	A	A C, D
10-30	1-12 (dummy)	B	B D
20-40	10-11 (real)	C A	C
20-30	12-13 (real)	D A, B	D
30-40	11-20 (dummy)		
	11-30 (dummy		
	13-30 (dummy)		
	20-21 (real)		
	30-31 (real)		
	21-40 (dummy)		
	31-40 (dummy)		

These can be read as follows:

Figure 1 & 2:
Activity 10-20 must be completed before activities 20-40 or 30-40 can be started.
Activity 10-30 must be completed before activity 30-40 can be started.
Activities 20-40 and 30-40 must be completed before the project can be declared completed.

Figure 3
The start of the project is denoted by event 1.
Dummy 1-10 must be marked completed before activity 10-11 can be started.
Dummy 1-12 must be marked completed before activity 12-13 can be started.
Activity 10-11 must be completed before dummies 11-20 and 11-30 can be marked completed.
Etc.

Figures 2, 3, & 4 (predecessor notation)
A has no predecessor and thus can start as soon as the project starts.
B has no predecessor and thus can start as soon as the project starts.
C cannot start until A is completed.
D cannot start until both A and B are completed.
The project is not completed until both C and D are completed.

Figures 3, 4, & 5 (follower notation)
A must be completed before C or D can start.
B must be completed before D can start.
C has no followers.
D has no followers.
The project is not completed until both C and D are completed.

TABLE IX.A.1

List Representations of Example Project Network Diagrams in Figure IX.A.1

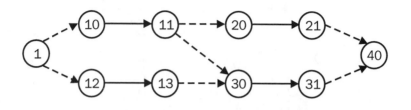

FIGURE IX.A.3

A Simple PEP Project Network Diagram

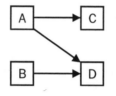

FIGURE IX.A.4

A Simple Activity-on-Node Project Network Diagram

system, especially in defense-related industries. It gravitated to CPM as users became less enamored with the three time estimates.

All of these were based on using directed graphs, more generally known as PNDs, as the basic language of planning. People soon referred to PERT charts, CPM charts, precedence charts, and logic diagrams as if they were the same and as if they were drastically different.

Eventually, the usage was so lax as to leave no precision in the use of any of these names. Soon the distinctions between these techniques became fuzzy, as practitioners and academicians used the terms differently *and* interchangeably. The ambiguity persists today, leading to confusion as to what technique, as well as what form of network diagramming, is meant. A clear understanding of these alternatives is important to further discussion.

It is also important to understand how each of these can be represented in tabular format. In Table IX.A.1, the tabular listings are shown for each of the earlier-referenced PNDS.

Epilogue

Herbert Simon, Nobel Laureate, once described the process of writing a book. He said something like, "You may think you know where you are going and what you are going to say, but soon the book takes on a personality and starts taking you into places you had not thought of." And so it does. Originally this book was conceived as a rather modest effort. It involved seventeen chapters that would explain the basic concepts and techniques of modern project management. Soon it was taking me into subjects of which I was aware but had not previously articulated in this context or at least to the same degree. Thus, the page count increased.

This posed a dilemma. When I was editor-in-chief for the Project Management Institute, I vowed that I would not publish a book of more than a couple hundred pages. On a trip to New York, I took a new book by Tom Peters, which included some six hundred pages. I still haven't finished it. It was too heavy for me to hold in one hand. It was too large for a briefcase with anything else in it. I was frustrated that I had not completed it. Thus, the vow.

So what started as *PM 101* has now become *PM 101* and *PM 102*. This current volume, *PM 101*, is small. It can be read on a plane, even while your meal tray is in front of you. Fast readers should certainly be able to finish it in one round trip of any distance. And, it just might fit into your pocket or purse.

In this volume, the concept of projects—as opposed to other modes of performing work—is explored. Modern project management is described, if not defined. The essential skills of a project manager are presented, and the process of defining a project and its plan are presented. If you, as a project manager, apply nothing more than the concepts and techniques presented in this book, you will improve your skills and your projects are more likely to be completed per requirements, on schedule, and within budget.

But you can do better yet. The project network diagram provides the framework for estimating and scheduling projects more precisely, considering resource availability, and managing cost, quality, and risk. It also provides a basis to design a reporting and control system that will encourage project team members to do the right things at the right time and correctly the first time. It is also important to understand the interrelatedness of all resources, not just people and equipment. These subjects will be presented in *PM 102*. You are encouraged to read it just as you might take a sequel course in a more formal learning environment.

Good luck, and may Murphy be kind to you.

References

Ansoff, Igor, ed. 1974. From Strategic Planning to Strategic Management.

Bartos, Ken, and William D. Brundage. 1989. The Voyager 2-Neptune Encounter, A Management Challenge: Speeding Toward Your Deadline at 42,000 Miles Per Hour ... Without Brakes. *PM Network* 3 (4): 7–23.

Bubna, Shashi K., and James J. Anderson. 1992. PM Meets the Challenge on Somincor's Neves-Corvo Tin Project. *PM Network* 6 (3): 9–22.

Dalal, Jagdish R., Suzanne M. DeSarra, David M. McEneany, and David M. Nowak. 1993. Improving Project Delivery and Resource Utilization. *PM Network* 7 (3): 11–15.

Darnall, Russell W. 1996. *The World's Greatest Project: One Project Team on the Path to Quality.* Upper Darby, PA: Project Management Institute.

Flones, Peter F. 1987. Endicott Oil Field: First Offshore Arctic Oil Field Begins Production. *Project Management Journal* 18 (5): 41–50.

Halli, Wayne. 1993. Scope Management Through a WBS: Key to Success for the Logan Expansion Project. *PM Network* (May): 12–18.

Hofstadter, Eva. 1992. The Science of the Deal: Project Management Meets Wall Street. *PM Network* 6 (8): 11–19.

Ibbs, C. William, and Young-Hoon Kwak. 1997. *The Benefits of Project Management.* Project Management Institute Educational Foundation.

Jet Propulsion Laboratory. 1998. Mars Pathfinder Project, submitted for PMI® Project of the Year. California Institute of Technology, with endorsement from the National Aeronautics and Space Administration, Washington, D. C.

Kelley, James E., Jr., and Morgan R. Walker. 1989. The Origins of CPM: A Personal History. *PM Network* 3 (2): 7–22.

Kerzner, Harold. 1989. Project Management: A Systems Approach to Planning, Scheduling and Control, 3d ed. New York: Van Nostrand Reinhold.

Lavold, Garry. 1983. Developing and Using the Work Breakdown Structure. In *Project Management Handbook,* edited by David I. Cleland and William R. King. New York: Van Nostrand Reinhold, 302–23.

Lemley, Jack K. 1992. The Channel Tunnel: Creating a Modern Wonder-of-the-World. *PM Network* 6 (5): 8–21.

Malcolm, D. G., J. H. Roseboom, C. E. Clark, and W. Fazar. 1959. Applications of a Technique for R&D Program Evaluation (PERT). *Operations Research* 7 (5): 646–69.

McCafferty, Dennis. 1998. Managing to Win. *USA Weekend* (April 24–26): 4–6.

Olde Curmudgeon, The. 1984. *Project Management Journal* 15 (June): 47–48.

———. 1993a. PM 101—Modern Project Management: A Concept Whose Time Has Come. *PM Network* 7 (3): 34–38.

———. 1993b. PM 101: So What Is a Project? *PM Network* 7 (6): 24–26, 28.

———. 1993c. PM 101: Project Management. *PM Network* 7 (9): 20–25.

———. 1993d. PM 101: The Project Manager—A Leader. *PM Network* 7 (12): 28–31.

———. 1994a. PM 101: The Project Manager—Technical Skills. *PM Network* 8 (3): 48–50.

———. 1994b. PM 101: The Project Manager—Administrative Skills. *PM Network* 8 (6): 33–36.

———. 1994c. PM 101: Scope Management. *PM Network* 8 (9): 38–40.

———. 1994d. PM 101: The WBS. *PM Network* 8 (12): 40–44, 46.

———. 1995. PM 101: Estimating. *PM Network* 9 (4): 42–47.

Ono, Dan. 1990. Implementing Project Management in AT&T's Business Communications System. *PM Network* 4 (7): 9–31.

PMBOK® Guide (A Guide to the Project Management Body of Knowledge). 1996. Upper Darby, PA: Project Management Institute, PMI Standards Committee.

Pearson, Randall. 1988. Project Management at the Minnesota Department of Transportation. *PM Network* (November): 7–19.

Peters, Tom. 1996. *Liberation Management*. Knopf.

———. 1998. *The Circle of Innovation: You Can't Shrink Your Way to Greatness*. Knopf.

Petersen, Normand. 1991. Selecting Project Managers: An Integrated List of Predictors. *Project Management Journal* 22 (2): 21–26.

Sandia National Laboratories. 1991. *The Preferred Processes—Project Planning and Management*. Albuquerque, New Mexico.

———. 1991. *Work Agreements: The Process for Getting Project Work Done*. Albuquerque, New Mexico (December): 11.

———. 1991. *Scope of Work Management*. Albuquerque, New Mexico (October): 10.

Swanton, Ronald E. 1988. Voyager. *Project Management Journal* (April): 33–48.

Snyder, John, and Bill Caligan. 1990. Bad Creek Pumped-Storage Hydro Station: Success by Many Measures. *PM Network* (August): 11–29.

Sparks, William O. 1993. A Case Study in Strategic Planning, Total Quality Management, and Project Management. *PM Network* 7 (3): 23–26.

Stanford University. 1964. *Documentation of the SPRED Program*, Stanford, CA.

Thamhain, Hans. 1991. Developing Project Management Skills. *Project Management Journal* 22 (3): 39–44.

TripMaker (computer CD). 1997. New York: Rand McNally.

Webster, F. M. 1993. *PM Network* Connection, A Plea for Clarity. *PM Network* (October): 41–42.

U.S. Air Force Systems Command. 1960. Documentation of the PEP Program, Wright-Patterson Air Base, Dayton, OH.

van Zyl, G. J. 1991. Sasol Market Share Enhanced: Record Breaking Polypropylene Project. *PM Network* 5 (8): 8–21.

Zells, Lois. 1993. Strategic Planning with Total Quality Management and Project Management. *PM Network* 7 (3): 17–21, 52–53.

Index

Upgrade Your Project Management Knowledge with First-Class Publications from PMI

THE PROJECT SPONSOR GUIDE

This to-the-point and quick reading for today's busy executives and managers is a one-of-a-kind source that describes the unique and challenging support that executives and managers must provide to be effective sponsors of project teams. *The Project Sponsor Guide* is intended for executives and middle managers who will be, or are, sponsors of a project, particularly cross-functional projects. It is also helpful reading for facilitators and project leaders.

ISBN: 1-880410-15-X (paperback)

DON'T PARK YOUR BRAIN OUTSIDE
A PRACTICAL GUIDE TO IMPROVING SHAREHOLDER VALUE WITH SMART MANAGEMENT

Don't Park Your Brain Outside is the thinking person's guide to extraordinary project performance. Francis Hartman has assembled a cohesive and balanced approach to highly effective project management. It is deceptively simple. Called SMART, this new approach is Strategically Managed, Aligned, Regenerative, and Transitional. It is based on research and best practices, tempered by hard-won experience. SMART has saved significant time and money on the hundreds of large and small, simple and complex projects on which it has been tested. Are your projects SMART? Find out by reading this people-oriented project management book with an attitude!

ISBN: 1-880410-48-6 (paperback)

THE ENTER*PRIZE* ORGANIZATION
ORGANIZING SOFTWARE PROJECTS FOR ACCOUNTABILITY AND SUCCESS

Every day project leaders are approached with haunting questions like: *What is the primary reason why projects fail? How technical should managers be? What are the duties of a project management office?* These haunting questions, along with many more, are just a few of the question and answers Whitten discusses in his latest book, *The Enter*Prize *Organization*. This book is for seasoned employees, as well as for those just entering the workforce. From beginning to end, you will recognize familiar ways to define the key project roles and responsibilities, and discover some new ideas in organizing a software project.

ISBN: 1-880410-79-6 (paperback)

A FRAMEWORK FOR PROJECT MANAGEMENT

This complete project management seminar course provides experienced project managers with an easy-to-use set of educational tools to help them deliver a seminar on basic project management concepts, tools, and techniques. *A Framework for Project Management* was developed and designed for seminar leaders by a team of experts within the PMI® membership, and reviewed extensively during its development and piloting stage by a team of PMPs.

ISBN: 1-880410-82-6 (Facilitator's Manual Set)
ISBN: 1-880410-80-X (Participant's Manual Set)

THE PMI PROJECT MANAGEMENT FACT BOOK

A comprehensive resource of information about PMI® and the profession it serves. Professionals working in project management require information and resources to function in today's global business environment. Knowledge along with data collection and interpretation are often key to determining success in the marketplace. The Project Management Institute (PMI®) anticipates the needs of the profession with *The PMI Project Management Fact Book*.

ISBN: 1-880410-62-1 (paperback)

PROJECT MANAGEMENT SOFTWARE SURVEY

The PMI® *Project Management Software Survey* offers an efficient way to compare and contrast the capabilities of a wide variety of project management tools. More than two hundred software tools are listed with comprehensive information on systems features; how they perform time analysis, resource analysis, cost analysis, performance analysis, and cost reporting; and how they handle multiple projects, project tracking, charting, and much more. The survey is a valuable tool to help narrow the field when selecting the best project management tools.

ISBN: 1-880410-52-4 (paperback)
ISBN: 1-880410-59-1 (CD-ROM)

THE JUGGLER'S GUIDE TO MANAGING MULTIPLE PROJECTS

This comprehensive book introduces and explains task-oriented, independent, and interdependent levels of project portfolios. It says that you must first have a strong foundation in time management and priority setting, then introduces the concept of Portfolio Management to timeline multiple projects, determine their resource requirements, and handle emergencies, putting you in charge for possibly the first time in your life!
ISBN: 1-880410-65-6 (paperback)

RECIPES FOR PROJECT SUCCESS

This book is destined to become "the" reference book for beginning project managers, particularly those who like to cook! Practical, logically developed project management concepts are offered in easily understood terms in a light-hearted manner. They are applied to the everyday task of cooking—from simple, single dishes, such as homemade tomato sauce for pasta, made from the bottom up, to increasingly complex dishes or meals for groups that in turn require an understanding of more complex project management terms and techniques. The transition between cooking and project management discussions is smooth, and tidbits of information provided with the recipes are interesting and humorous.
ISBN: 1-880410-58-3 (paperback)

TOOLS AND TIPS FOR TODAY'S PROJECT MANAGER

This guidebook is valuable for understanding project management and performing to quality standards. Includes project management concepts and terms—old and new—that are not only defined but also are explained in much greater detail than you would find in a typical glossary. Also included are tips on handling such seemingly simple everyday tasks as how to say "No" and how to avoid telephone tag. It's a reference you'll want to keep close at hand.
ISBN: 1-880410-61-3 (paperback)

THE FUTURE OF PROJECT MANAGEMENT

The project management profession is going through tremendous change—both evolutionary and revolutionary. Some of these changes are internally driven, while many are externally driven. Here, for the first time, is a composite view of some major trends occurring throughout the world and the implication of them on the profession of project management and on the Project Management Institute. Read the views of the 1998 PMI Research Program Team, a well-respected futurist firm, and other authors. This book represents the beginning of a journey and, through inputs from readers and others, it will continue as a work in progress.
ISBN: 1-880410-71-0 (paperback)

NEW RESOURCES FOR PMP CANDIDATES

The following publications are resources that certification candidates can use to gain information on project management theory, principles, techniques, and procedures.

PMP RESOURCE PACKAGE

Earned Value Project Management
by Quentin W. Fleming and Joel M. Koppelman

Effective Project Management: How to Plan, Manage, and Deliver Projects on Time and Within Budget
by Robert K. Wysocki, et al.

A Guide to the Project Management Body of Knowledge (PMBOK® Guide)
by the PMI Standards Committee

Human Resource Skills for the Project Manager
by Vijay K. Verma

The New Project Management
by J. Davidson Frame

Organizing Projects for Success
by Vijay K. Verma

Principles of Project Management
by John Adams, et al.

Project & Program Risk Management
by R. Max Wideman, Editor

Project Management Casebook
edited by David I. Cleland, et al.

Project Management: A Managerial Approach, Fourth Edition
by Jack R. Meredith and Samuel J. Mantel Jr.

Project Management: A Systems Approach to Planning, Scheduling, and Controlling, Sixth Edition
by Harold Kerzner

A GUIDE TO THE PROJECT MANAGEMENT BODY OF KNOWLEDGE (PMBOK® GUIDE)

The basic management reference for everyone who works on projects. Serves as a tool for learning about the generally accepted knowledge and practices of the profession. As "management by projects" becomes more and more a recommended business practice worldwide, the *PMBOK® Guide* becomes an essential source of information that should be on every manager's bookshelf. Available in hardcover or paperback, the *PMBOK® Guide* is an official standards document of the Project Management Institute.
ISBN: 1-880410-12-5 (paperback), ISBN: 1-880410-13-3 (hardcover)